EFFECTIVE PROJECT PLANNING
AND MANAGEMENT

W. Alan Randolph
University of South Carolina

Barry Z. Posner
Santa Clara University

EFFECTIVE PROJECT PLANNING AND MANAGEMENT
Getting the Job Done

Prentice Hall, Englewood Cliffs, New Jersey 07632

Library of Congress Cataloging-in-Publication Data

Randolph, W. Alan
    Effective project planning and management.

    Bibliography: p.
    Includes index.
    1. Industrial project management.   I. Posner, Barry Z.
    II. Title.
    HD69.P75R36 1987   658.4'04   87-11399
    ISBN 0-13-244815-7

Fairleigh Dickinson
University Library,

Teaneck, New Jersey

Editorial/production supervision
    and interior design: **Cheryl Lynn Smith**
Cover design: **Ben Santora**
Manufacturing buyers: **Margaret Rizzi/Paula Benevento**

The publisher offers discounts on this book when ordered
in bulk quantities. For more information, write:

    Special Sales/College Marketing
    Prentice Hall
    College Technical and Reference Division
    Englewood Cliffs, New Jersey 07632

Printed in the United States of America

10 9 8 7 6 5 4 3 2

ISBN   0-13-244815-7   025

Prentice-Hall International (UK) Limited, *London*
Prentice-Hall of Australia Pty. Limited, *Sydney*
Prentice-Hall Canada Inc., *Toronto*
Prentice-Hall Hispanoamericana, S.A., *Mexico*
Prentice-Hall of India Private Limited, *New Delhi*
Prentice-Hall of Japan, Inc., *Tokyo*
Simon & Schuster Asia Pte. Ltd., *Singapore*
Editora Prentice-Hall do Brasil, Ltda., *Rio de Janeiro*

To Our Wives
Ruth Anne
and
Jackie

CONTENTS

CONTENTS

EFFECTIVE PROJECT PLANNING AND MANAGEMENT

WHY READ THIS BOOK?

WHY READ THIS BOOK?

- Does your job require you to finish assignments by a specified deadline?
- Do you have more than one task to accomplish during the day?
- Do you have to get your various tasks completed with a limited set of resources?
- Do you have to work with other people in order to get your own work done?
- Do you always know what the end result of your work will look like?
- Do your supervisors, colleagues, or customers ever change their mind about what they want?

If you answered yes to these questions, you are a project manager. Regardless of job titles, almost everyone has responsibilities for managing projects. And all of us have felt that we could manage projects (assignments, tasks, duties, programs, promotions, campaigns, products, accounts) better than we have in the past.

Many books have been written about management, but few of them focus on MANAGING PROJECTS and GETTING THE JOB DONE. Most books talk about "shoulds," like "we should drain the swamp." But we all know how hard it is to focus on the swamp reclamation project when we are "up to our rear ends dealing with the alligators!" This book will tell you how to "train" those alligators; how to manage your projects to successful completion; how to GET THE JOB DONE.

Let's look at how you manage your projects. Check "yes" or "no"

for the following ten questions. Be honest with yourself. Can you really
say yes to these questions, or do you only wish you could?

__ __ Do you have a clear idea of what you are trying to accomplish
         for the project user? (Rule Number One)
__ __ Can you articulate the constraints and directives that govern
         your project? (Rule Number Two)
__ __ Is your project broken down into manageable chunks? (Rule
         Number Three)
__ __ Do you have a written schedule for your project? (Rule Number
         Four)
__ __ Do you understand the perspectives of the people whose work
         affects your project? (Rule Number Five)
__ __ Are others excited about and committed to success on the
         project? (Rule Number Six)
__ __ Do you listen more than you talk? (Rule Number Seven)
__ __ When disagreements arise, can you build effective agreements?
         (Rule Number Eight)
__ __ Do others willingly follow your requests? (Rule Number Nine)
__ __ Can you get people to be imaginative and creative on the
         project? (Rule Number Ten)
YES NO

These questions relate to the ten rules for GETTING THE JOB DONE.
Each chapter of this book explains what it takes to answer yes to these
questions. How many times did you check "yes"? _____ . You can
interpret your score on the next page.

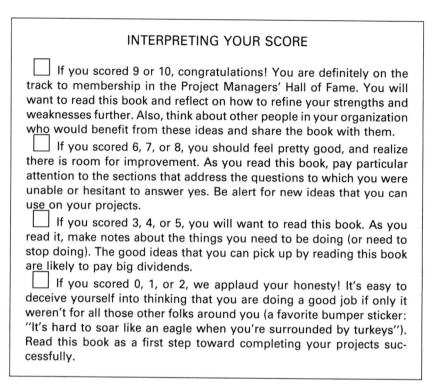

INTERPRETING YOUR SCORE

☐ If you scored 9 or 10, congratulations! You are definitely on the track to membership in the Project Managers' Hall of Fame. You will want to read this book and reflect on how to refine your strengths and weaknesses further. Also, think about other people in your organization who would benefit from these ideas and share the book with them.

☐ If you scored 6, 7, or 8, you should feel pretty good, and realize there is room for improvement. As you read this book, pay particular attention to the sections that address the questions to which you were unable or hesitant to answer yes. Be alert for new ideas that you can use on your projects.

☐ If you scored 3, 4, or 5, you will want to read this book. As you read it, make notes about the things you need to be doing (or need to stop doing). The good ideas that you can pick up by reading this book are likely to pay big dividends.

☐ If you scored 0, 1, or 2, we applaud your honesty! It's easy to deceive yourself into thinking that you are doing a good job if only it weren't for all those other folks around you (a favorite bumper sticker: "It's hard to soar like an eagle when you're surrounded by turkeys"). Read this book as a first step toward completing your projects successfully.

WHY WE WROTE THIS BOOK

We wrote this book to help people become better managers of projects. Since 1980 we have been providing seminars and consulting services on EFFECTIVE PROJECT PLANNING AND MANAGEMENT throughout the country. We have learned a great deal from studying hundreds of projects in a variety of organizations. We have learned from the actual experiences of thousands of people who manage all kinds of projects. And we have learned from the more than 10,000 people nationwide who have participated in our seminars. Through our discussions with managers and our studies of project management, we have identified effective ways to plan and manage projects. Reading this book, you will pick up proven ideas that will save you time, aggravation, and money. *Effective Project Planning and Management: Getting the Job Done* is about managing projects to successful completion.

Introduction

EVERYONE MANAGES PROJECTS

EVERYONE MANAGES PROJECTS

Every one of us is a manager of projects! From production employee to financial analyst, from banker to physician, from engineer to administrator, we all work on various tasks with deadlines. Regardless of our occupation, discipline, or location in an organization, we all work on tasks that are unique and involve people who do not usually work together. The project may have a simple objective that does not require many people or a great deal of money, or it may be quite complex, calling for diverse skills and many resources. Typically, projects share most if not all of the six characteristics listed in Figure A on page 10.

Managing a project to successful completion can be a challenge. It's like being a race car driver. Imagine that you are on a race track. Your crew is not used to working together. The competition is fierce. The course has many blind curves. You want to be the first to receive the checkered flag, signaling completion of the race. This is the opportunity of a lifetime. If you do a good job of managing the project—if you can win the race—your success is out in the open for others to see. Of course, if you do not get the job done right, that result is also out in the open. The stakes are high: win or lose. Yet the opportunity to "show your stuff" is not one to miss.

Characteristics of a Project

1. A start and a finish

2. A time frame for completion

3. A unique one-timeness

4. An involvement of several people
   on an ad-hoc basis

5. A limited set of resources

6. A sequencing of activities and
   phases

Figure A

HOW TO MANAGE PROJECTS
TO SUCCESSFUL COMPLETION

Good project managers make things happen. And when they do, people notice! What is their secret to success? The bottom line is that effective managers of projects get the job done *on time, within budget*, and *according to desired quality standards*.

Effective project managers take the time necessary to plan their projects and to manage that plan well. Too often, people try to complete a project without a plan. They use a "let's fix it in the field" mentality; it should come as no surprise that others pass them by. Effective managers of projects appreciate the need to go slow at first, so they can go fast later. No project ever goes 100 percent according to plan, but you will have a better idea what to do when things go astray if you go slow at first. Good planning leads to *smaller* problems during implementation and allows you to go faster later.

Effective project managers involve a large number of people in the planning process. They ask a lot of questions like "What if this happens?" and "What could go wrong?" This means you'll need to develop a strong sense of agreement and commitment from your people. Make certain that all of the functional groups and organizational layers involved in implementing the project plan are "signed up."

Effective project managers know when to stop planning and when to move into action. You will need to develop a sense for when the planning group has exhausted the "What if?" and "What could go wrong?" questions. And you'll need to understand how to find a common ground, enabling project participants to work through their inevitable disagreements.

Effective project managers employ their power to lead the project through to implementation. You will need to understand how to develop credibility and be able to unleash people's creative energies.

THE RULES FOR MANAGING PROJECTS

The rules for project success are not the providence of a divine few. We learned them from our studies of effective project managers. And across the country, people who have attended our seminars have helped us to develop and refine these ten rules:

1. Set a clear project **G**oal.
2. Determine the project **O**bjectives.
3. Establish **C**heckpoints, **A**ctivities, **R**elationships, and **T**ime estimates.
4. Draw a picture of the project **S**chedule.
5. **D**irect people individually and as a project team.
6. **R**einforce the commitment and excitement of the project team.
7. Keep everyone connected with the project **I**nformed.
8. Build agreements that **V**italize team members.
9. **E**mpower yourself and others on the project team.
10. Encourage **R**isk taking and creativity.

The boldfaced letters in the first four rules spell GO-CARTS. This is our acronym for building a good plan. Effective project managers build good plans—GO-CARTS—to get them from the start of the race to the finish line.

Even the best-built GO-CARTS, however, will not produce a winner without a skillful driver. And that's what the boldfaced letters in the last six rules spell: DRIVER. This is our acronym for what needs to happen as you implement your plan, not necessarily in a particular order but as required in the life of the project. When you know how to build effective GO-CARTS and how to be a skillful DRIVER, you can get your projects over the finish line without crashing. So let's take a closer look at the rules for building your GO-CARTS and developing your skills as a DRIVER.

1

Rule Number One

SET A CLEAR
PROJECT GOAL

SET A CLEAR PROJECT GOAL

What is the desired end result of your project? Its scope? Its goal? Amazingly, most people managing a project cannot readily answer these questions! John Young, Hewlett-Packard's chief executive officer and chairperson of President Reagan's Commission on Productivity, referred to this as the challenge of "doing the right thing versus doing things right." Consider the famous example from *Alice in Wonderland* (Figure 1.1 on page 16.): If you don't know where you're going, any road will get you there!

In getting the job done, you must mentally start at the finish . . . and work backward. The clearer you are about the end result of your project, even though it may change, the more effectively you can plan the best way to achieve it.

Ever worked a jigsaw puzzle? You've got a thousand pieces to the puzzle—all the necessary resources to complete the project. How do you begin? By looking at the cover of the puzzle box. By studying the picture of what the pieces will look like once they are assembled properly. You start at the end result and plan backward to the beginning. Then you begin to work toward the final goal.

Since most of your projects require the involvement of other people, having a clear goal and being able to articulate it to others is essential. If the project team lacks a clear goal, even excellent skills and the best equipment will not enable the team to do a good job.

For example, give a highly skilled archer the best equipment available and tell her to start shooting, but don't tell her where the target is.

From Alice in Wonderland

"Cheshire Puss, " she began, rather timidly, as she
did not at all know whether it would like the name:
however, it only grinned a little wider. "Come, it's
pleased so far, " thought Alice, and she went on.
"Would you please tell me, please, which way I ought
to go from here?"
   "That depends a good deal on where you want to
get to," said the Cat.
   "I don't much care where" said Alice.
   "Then it doesn't matter which way you go," said
the Cat.
   "So long as I get somewhere," Alice added as an
explanation.
   "Oh, you're sure to do that," said the Cat, "if you
only walk long enough."

Figure 1.1

The archer shoots the arrows where she thinks is appropriate, but not at
the target you had in mind. It's not that the archer isn't trying; she just
does not know where to aim. She soon winds up frustrated in her efforts,
and you are disappointed in the results. Time and energy are wasted. The
archer has wasted her expertise and the money you've spent for her fine
equipment. Whose fault is this? *Yours.*

If you don't point your people in the right direction, if you don't
give them the big picture (show them the picture on the jigsaw puzzle
box), if you can't get them to imagine how they would feel using the
product or service (the end result of your project), you are locked into
an activity trap! People will be busy spinning their wheels, but nothing
significant will be getting accomplished. Your team may have all the
skills and equipment, but they don't know where the target is. This is
called "running a well-managed bankruptcy"!

SETTING PROJECT GOALS

Many project managers, as well as their supervisors in upper management,
think it is easy to set goals—just state them. But it is not easy. It's hard
work. It's also the most important action you can take at the beginning
of a project. What does it take to set a good project goal?

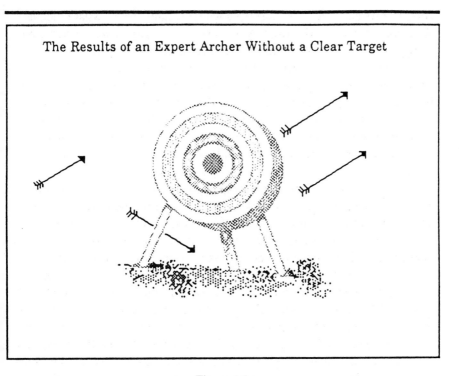

The Results of an Expert Archer Without a Clear Target

Figure 1.2

In setting a project goal, you are trying to do two things: (1) to focus yourself and your team on the target and (2) to create commitment and agreement about the project goal. From where does this clarity of focus come?

Project managers complain that they cannot get direction from upper management. We have often heard people say that upper management can state what they do *not* want, but not *what* they want. This is a cop-out. Goal clarification is the result of the *process* of goal setting. And it is this process that takes time, energy, and dialogue. It is a process of going back and forth with other people, working toward a clarity of direction for the project.

Since each project tends to be unique—it is not something that has been done before—it is difficult to be clear on a goal right away. And since goal setting is a process of dialogue, it can start in one of two ways: Top management or customers tell you what to do, or you tell top management what you see as the goal for a project. You write it down on a piece of paper and say, "Here, this is what I think the project goal is." And that gives management the option to say, "Yes, I agree. That's correct. Proceed'' or ''No, that's not what I meant. Here's what I meant.'' And you go back and forth as you move closer and closer to achieving clarity about the direction and the end result of the project.

The best way to capture the project goal is in a statement of project results: How will we know we are finished? What will the end result look like? Effective project managers do this by stating their goals in *user terms*. Think about this for a moment. Who is the user of your project? *What* does your user—client, customer, account, patient, or manager— want from you? What does the end user say you are supposed to be doing?

A user doesn't care, for example, that you are trying to produce a new accounting system (one ineffective way to describe a project's goal). The user cares about obtaining certain information about inventory and sales at the end of the day. Providing a system that meets the user's needs is your goal; designing a new accounting system is your process for doing this. Putting yourself on the user's side improves your chances of hitting the target. And if you can't identify a use for your project, why are you doing it? The gods punished Sisyphus by giving him the task of pushing a boulder to a mountaintop, only to have it roll back down to the bottom, where Sisyphus had to begin again. You don't want to be like Sisyphus.

Effective managers of projects always try to involve the end user directly in the project, or at least to imagine the user's point of view. This is the customer perspective. Research studies point out that users originate most major technological innovations. For example, the people at Stew Leonard's phenomenally successful grocery store in Norwalk, Connecticut, have made their customers the boss. Several customers had complained that the fish wasn't fresh. This wasn't true, but the customers perceived that fish packaged in cellophane and styrofoam trays wasn't fresh. So Leonard built a fresh fish box, where fish would be purchased ''fresh'' off the ice. He didn't notice any fall-off in his sales of packaged fresh fish, but he started selling 100 percent more fish fresh off the ice! As Leonard explains, ''Nobody comes into my store to make Stew Leonard happy. If we don't make the customers feel happy, they won't come here. And why should they? I wouldn't!''

"SMART" GOALS

In addition to establishing a goal in terms of the user, an effective project goal has five characteristics. These characteristics are captured in the term SMART, an acronym for the aspects of a goal that is likely to provide focus and create commitment. SMART goals are specific, **m**easurable, **a**greed upon, **r**ealistic, and **t**ime-framed.

Specific.   Your goal should be so **specific**, so well defined, so clear that anybody with some basic knowledge of the project area can read it, understand it, and know what you are trying to accomplish. You could drop dead tomorrow (of course, we do not recommend that you test it this way) and somebody else could pick up the statement of your project's goals and know exactly what to do. It should be that clearly defined.

Measurable.   To manage a project to successful completion, you have to be able to **measure** what the goal is. It's been said—*wrongly*— that some project goals cannot be measured. But every goal that can be written down can be measured. Of course, some goals can be measured more easily than others. In fact, developing clear measuring standards for the more ambiguous and fuzzy kinds of goals is where you should spend the most time. Without measurable goals, project team members cannot get any sense of direction, and they wind up like the archer— shooting at the wrong target. Project participants need to work on measurable activities, even if the measures are crude, in order to know what to do. And you need a measurable goal if you are to manage it.

> Every goal can be measured,
> it's just that some goals
> can be measured more easily
> than others.

Figure 1.3

For example, Ken Blanchard, co-author of *The One Minute Manager*, describes how a large bank wanted to create an image of friendliness, but nobody knew how to measure friendliness. Top management felt that bank personnel were not friendly, and a survey of customers confirmed this feeling. The consultants called in to work with the bank decided, after much discussion with bank personnel, to measure friendliness by counting the number of comments between customers and bank personnel unrelated to work—comments about the weather, about how somebody was dressed, or about how cousin Johnny was feeling these days. The consultants found that very few of the comments between bank personnel and their customers were of this non-task-related variety (about one comment per customer interaction). The goal of the "friendliness project'' was to increase the number of non-task-related comments per interaction from one to four. All bank personnel got involved. They talked about the goal with the consultants, they discussed examples of what to say, and they worked at it. After five weeks of observing, the consultants determined that the number of non-task-related comments per interaction had risen to four. A follow-up customer survey revealed that their perception of the bank's friendliness had gone up dramatically. This is not a particularly brilliant measure of friendliness, but it worked. It gave people a target they could aim at. They could also measure their own progress. Having clear measuring standards is a vital part of the process of setting good goals.

Agreed upon.   There must be **agreement** about the project's goals. The end user, be it a customer, upper management, or a subordinate in the organization, must agree that the project goal is desirable. Stated differently, the project manager and the project's ''customer'' must agree that the end result should solve the problem or respond to the need that led to the initiation of the project. The more that people agree and have clarified the goal up front, the easier it will be to develop a viable plan for the project. This agreement will make it easier to respond to changes that may require modifying the goal as the project unfolds. Agreement is based on sharing information, and it builds commitment toward the project.

Realistic.   Project goals must be **realistic**. All too often project managers set goals that are impossible to achieve, given the resources, knowledge, and time available. Such project managers set themselves up for frustration. How many times have you been assigned a project and a deadline before the goal is clarified, only to find out that the project cannot possibly be completed on time? One of the benefits you derive from dialogue in the goal-setting process is determining whether you are talking about a goal that is realistic, given your resources. You have to question this assumption explicitly. Don't just say, ''Sure, we can get that done.'' Discuss resources, personnel, and timing to determine how realistic the goal is. Making it realistic may mean adjusting the goal, the deadline, or the resources.

Realism also means that even though the project is unique and different from what you have done before, it should not be totally alien to project personnel. If it is, you are asking for trouble. In this case you will need to set aside time for research and learning, or perhaps engage consultants or hire new project members or even delay the project. You should not get trapped into doing things you know little about, unless you want to fail. This is the wisdom of "stick to your knitting," which successful companies follow. Do the things you have some experience with. The goal-setting process should help you to clarify this issue.

Time-framed.   Finally, you need a clear **time frame** for the goal. How much time and budget do you have to accomplish this project? Is there any flexibility in the deadline? Is there any flexibility in the resources available for the project? This goes back to looking at what is attainable. You want to set a deadline that is reasonable, given the resources available and the amount of knowledge and experience you have with this type of project.

> **SMART Goals**
>
> A back-and-forth process to clarify direction and commitment.
>
> **Goal setting takes time and energy!**

Figure 1.4

Consider, for example, the project that God gave to Noah. God's voice boomed, "Build an ark of gopher wood, 300 cubits long, 50 cubits wide, and 30 cubits high. And do it in seven months, when I will destroy the earth by flood. Take a male and female of every animal; we are starting over."

Was that goal specific? Yes. Measurable? Not too clear on the animals but clear on the ark. Agreed upon? Who can argue with God? Noah believed in God, hence he accepted the goal. Realistic? Yes; Noah was a fisherman who knew about boats. Time-framed? Yes; rains were to begin in seven months. But we can imagine some discussion between Noah and God about the project planning—Noah questioning God on size, type of wood, animals to be excluded, why the flood; and God explaining and refining the goal until Noah is completely clear about it. Perhaps you have similar discussions with your supervisors. The question to ask is, does your project have a SMART goal?

Take a few minutes to write down the goal for one of your projects. Then check it against the standards of the SMART criteria. Have you written a SMART goal? Is it specific, measurable, agreed upon, realistic, and time-framed?

The importance of spending the necessary time and energy on the goal-setting process cannot be overemphasized. Effective goal setting is crucial for your projects because it provides a common vision that gives members of the team a sense of ownership. Clear goals build excitement.

Once you have a SMART project goal, you must make it a common vision for every member of the project team. You need to keep everyone's eyes focused on that target until it is achieved. There are a number of things you can do to facilitate this. The first is to write the goal down. A written goal distributed to everybody on your team will prevent team members from losing sight of the goal. You should also constantly remind people that *this* is the project goal—*this* is what we are all trying to accomplish. One of the primary responsibilities of the project manager is to keep the overall vision of the goal squarely in front of project personnel. You need to be sure that people on the project team always know what they are trying to accomplish for the person or group who will use their product. Doing this improves communication, reduces tension, allows team members to evaluate if they are contributing to the goal, and ensures that your project will be completed successfully.

CONCLUSION

Project planning begins with the end result—the goal—and works backward. Clarify what you are trying to accomplish for the user and always keep it uppermost in mind. Effective project managers always keep their eyes on the goal and make sure that everybody else on the project team is aimed in the same direction.

A SMART goal is an essential tool for motivating people on the project because it gives them the information and the perspective they need to keep the project moving in the proper direction. Effective project managers develop the goal, ensure that it is clear, communicate it to all of their people, create a commitment to it, and make certain that project team members are constantly aware of it and constantly working toward it. If you can create this common vision, every member of the project team can focus in the same direction. This first step in building a vehicle to drive you to the checkered flag is extremely important. It is the *G* in your GO-CART (summarized in Figure 1.5).

The G in GO-CART

Effective Project Managers:

- Develop the project goal
- Make sure it is clear and SMART
- Communicate it to all team members
- Keep the goal constantly out in front of people

Figure 1.5

2

Rule Number Two

DETERMINE THE PROJECT OBJECTIVES

DETERMINE THE PROJECT OBJECTIVES

Once you have gone through the goal-setting process and have a clear idea of where the project is going, you are ready to move ahead. You are ready to add more detail to your project because clearly you cannot operate simply with a goal. Noah, for example, needed more detail than just the command "Build an ark." So does your project team. You must add the **O** to GO-CARTS and establish **O**bjectives.

Objectives are guiding principles that direct the efforts of team members in their contribution to the project's goal. Generally speaking, you need an objective for each functional group associated with the project or, in some cases, for each person involved in the project. Team members need to know how each person will contribute to the project. Objectives are similar to goals, but they are focused on each group in the project. They break down the project goal and commit each group to a specific task that helps to accomplish the ultimate project goal. They tell each group or person what to do, when to do it, and how to measure progress. In essence, the project objectives are subparts of the overall project goal. Accomplishment of each particular objective leads to the overall project goal (Figure 2.1 on page 28.).

If, for example, your project is to install a new computer system, you would assign Group 1 the objective of preparing the site for the computer, Group 2 the responsibility (the objective) of getting the computer ordered and delivered to the installation site, Group 3 the responsibility of wiring the computer, and Group 4 the responsibility of debugging

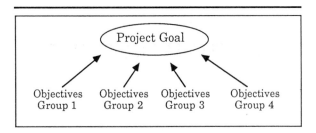

Figure 2.1

the computer to make it operate as designed. Once these objectives are reached, your project team has completed the goal of installing a new computer system on the user's premises.

In essence, objectives resemble goals. But objectives focus on the details and tell you more about what specific people need to accomplish. They set a target for each of the various groups involved in a project. Just as with the goal of the project, you must use a back-and-forth process to establish clear, well-defined objectives. You can apply the SMART criteria to each objective. An objective must be specific, measurable, agreed upon, realistic, and time-framed. Otherwise, objectives cannot guide the behavior of project participants effectively.

> Objectives, like goals,
> need to be SMART.
> They also need to be
> more narrowly defined.

Figure 2.2

Once you have a clear statement of project objectives, you need to identify the key project team members, resources, and inputs necessary to accomplish the overall project goal. By identifying each objective with a specific group (or a specific individual) and having a dialogue about its formulation, you establish ownership. Ownership leads people to take responsibility and feel committed to accomplishing the objective.

Everyone has a responsibility and must own up to that fact. Each person should understand how fulfilling that responsibility ties into the overall project goal. Many manufacturing organizations have begun to recognize this process. They are redesigning their production flow so that each person feels less like a small cog in the machinery and more like an essential contributor to the production process. People who help formulate their objectives tend to be more committed to accomplishing them. As Ray Abuzayyad, president of Rolm Corporation and vice-president of IBM, says, "You can't do it all by yourself. You must have a team." And objectives define the role of each team member's contribution to the overall project goal.

Just as you did for the project goal, put the project objectives in writing and literally hang them on the wall. That way they constantly remind each individual and each project group of what it is trying to accomplish. Signetics made a companywide commitment to zero defects, and everyone signed a pledge to achieve zero defects. Each of these signed statements was displayed on the lobby walls of the corporate offices. Signetics eventually *guaranteed* perfection in its shipments to all its customers.

And what about Noah and his ark? What are some of the objectives that Noah established to achieve his primary goal? Several possibilities are shown in Figure 2.3. Noah took the overall goal of building an ark and began to specify the responsibilities of the different functional groups that had to contribute to its completion.

Clarity of objectives is essential to effective project performance. Research on peak-performing individuals and groups in organizations suggests that they are always clear about their objectives. They know

---

Noah's Ark Project
(Sample Objectives)

Objectives for woodcutters:
>   Cut 600 pieces of gopher wood, each 10 feet long by 1 foot wide by 3 inches thick. Have this done in two months.

Objectives for carpenters:
>   Take the 600 pieces of gopher wood and fit them together into an ark 300 cubits long, 50 cubits wide, and 30 cubits high. Do this in three months.

Objectives for the animal handlers:
>   Find the best-looking and strongest male and female of each species of animal. No rejects, please. Get them here in two months.

Figure 2.3

where they are headed. And this sense of direction substantially increases their chances of getting there.

PROBLEMS IN SETTING OBJECTIVES

As with goal setting, many people are not very good at setting project objectives. Objectives should be designed so that their accomplishment leads to achievement of the project goal. But as you know, there are times when it just does not work out that way. Why does this occur?

Focusing Too Narrowly

Objectives alone are not enough. You must look at what tends to happen as your project personnel begin to work on their objectives. The objectives become their focus day in and day out, and it is easy for them to lose sight of the end result or project goal. It is also very easy for a group to lose sight of the objectives of the other groups working on the project. Project personnel readily go off on a tangent or accomplish their objectives in a way that makes it more difficult for the other team members to accomplish their objectives.

Project personnel get lost in the detail of their objectives and lose sight of the big picture—the project goal. In other words, they fail to recognize the forest through all the trees. Manufacturing builds a product that can't be marketed on a cost-effective basis. Marketing promises customized products when operations are based on a mass-production system. The key to avoiding too narrow a focus is to keep the project goal out in the open. As a project manager, you must constantly remind team members of the project goal to combat the tendency to focus too narrowly.

Reward Systems

Reward systems in most organizations tend to push team members apart. Instead of fostering cooperation to achieve the project goal, they create competitiveness between groups as each works on its own objectives. Typically, reward systems focus on the accomplishment of the objectives for each functional group and not on the accomplishment of the project goal.

A good example of this breakdown occurred at a naval air station that had four squadrons responsible for the maintenance of planes. The stated goal was to have 95 percent of all planes ready to go at any time. Actual readiness was running around 85 percent. The new commanding officer decided he would reassert this goal of 95 percent and backed it up with a reward system. Each month, he would give the particular squadron with the highest percentage of planes a reward, such as a 24-hour pass or public recognition of a job well done. What happened?

The members of one squadron decided that the secret was to have a well-stocked parts inventory. Then if a plane came in with a broken radar part, they could simply take that part out and put in a replacement and the plane would be ready to go again. They also realized that if they could increase their parts inventory while decreasing the parts inventory for the other squadrons, they would be well on the way to winning this competition. The obvious solution? Steal parts! This may sound ridiculous, but it is a true story.

One of the squadrons began to engage in midnight requisitions to steal parts from the other squadrons. The other squadrons figured out what was going on and decided to retaliate. Soon four squadrons were stealing from one another. Every squadron put guards on duty 24 hours a day, seven days a week to protect its inventories. Meanwhile, the percentage of planes ready to go was going downhill fast.

The problem was the reward system. People knew the overall project goal but felt that their own squadron's objectives were more important, especially since these objectives were what was being rewarded. A simple change in the reward system solved the problem. In a given month, any squadron that achieved the goal of 95 percent readiness would get the reward. Now, every squadron could get the reward. What happened? First of all, the stealing stopped. The squadrons started sharing parts to help one another out. The readiness percentage quickly rose to 90 percent and began pushing toward 95 percent—all because the reward system was changed to support the accomplishment of the objectives *and* the project goal.

As a project manager, you can't set the objectives and then forget about them. An ancient Chinese proverb captures this well: "People do

"People do not what
the manager <u>expects</u>
but what the manager
<u>inspects</u> and <u>rewards</u>."

Figure 2.4

not what the manager expects, but what the manager inspects''—or, in this case, what the manager rewards. It is foolish to expect a result when you are not rewarding it but are rewarding something else. If you want people to cooperate on a project and to keep the overall project goal in mind, you will have to reward their efforts toward the project goal. See Figure 2.4 on page 31.

Responsibility but Not Enough Authority

The concept of rewards related to objectives can also help you understand why project managers often have responsibility but lack authority. Think about the typical setup of a project. Suppose the new company computer will affect four departments—data processing, accounting, production, and sales. Within each department, people report to the department manager. Several of these people also report to the project manager in charge of the new computer system changeover. Thus they have two bosses—their department manager and the project manager. The project accounts for half their responsibilities, departmental matters the other half. But who evaluates these people at the end of the year? The project manager? No. The department manager. So if there is any conflict in what the two managers tell the employee to do, what will the employee do? Ignore or put off the project manager.

For the project manager approach to be successful, each person or functional group involved in the project's success must agree to cooperate

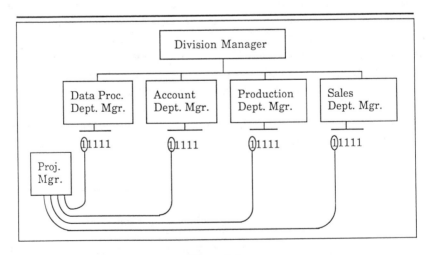

Figure 2.5

and to coordinate efforts so that no employee is asked to do two things at the same time. And the project manager must have input into the evaluation of the employee (generally 50-50 with the department manager in this example, since half of the person's work is on the project). When team members know that both managers will be engaged in evaluating their performance, they are motivated to do what both managers say.

But we must go one step further and ask how we can get the data processing, accounting, production, and sales managers to cooperate with the project manager? In many cases, department managers have no real accountability for a project. But in companies where the project manager approach works best, department managers are held partly responsible for the success of the project. The division manager evaluates department managers not only in terms of department activities but also in terms of how well the project is succeeding. The department managers have a reason to cooperate and work with the project manager. Each individual department manager has a stake in the project and knows that rewards and evaluations depend on project success. The department managers focus not only on the project objectives involving their department but also on the overall success of the project. The department managers tend to cooperate and coordinate with one another and with the project manager.

Now, your organization may not have this kind of formalized project accountability for department managers. But if it does not, don't just throw up your hands. Instead, use the informal organization. Go outside the hierarchy to develop a relationship with each of the department managers and draw them into the project. Get them on your side and make them understand how you are going to help them. In other words, depend on a relationship with the department managers.

For example, Judy Randal is a marketing analyst for a large oil company. To complete her projects, she has to get information from salespeople in the field, but she has no authority over them. To go through the organizational channels up several levels, across, and then down several levels to ask a sales rep to provide information would take months. And the sales reps have no stake in Judy's project. So Judy works on her relationship with the salespeople. In fact, she goes out and rides the territory with the sales reps, talks with them, and gets to know them. Then, when she calls up to ask for information, it is not just the marketing analyst calling, it is their friend Judy. So even though the system may not support you by coordinating the objectives of different departments, you can ensure that those objectives tie in to the project goal by working through the informal organization.

CONCLUSION

Developing SMART objectives that tie in to the project goal is not easy. It takes time and energy, and it takes the cooperation of all parties involved. Furthermore, you must continually focus on objectives as they relate to the project goal and link rewards to accomplishment of the project goal.

Earlier you wrote down a goal for one of your projects. Take a few moments to write an objective for each the groups or individuals who must assist you with your project. Tell your team exactly what has to be done, the time frame, and who will do what, and state your objectives in a way that is measurable. Are your objectives SMART?

The "O" in GO-CART

A good project manager continually focuses team members on how objectives relate to the overall project goal and links rewards to the overall goal.

Figure 2.6

3

Rule Number Three

ESTABLISH CHECKPOINTS, ACTIVITIES, RELATIONSHIPS, AND TIME ESTIMATES

Rule Number Three

ESTABLISH CHECKPOINTS, ACTIVITIES, RELATIONSHIPS, AND TIME ESTIMATES

It is not enough to have a goal and objectives; you need checkpoints and activities to get your project to the goal and objectives. Otherwise, how can you tell if you are going in the right direction? How will you know when to slow down or speed things up? How will you know how much time you will need? You must add further detail to your plan by assembling the vehicle that will take you to the finish line and enable you to get the job done.

GO may be your propellant, but you will need a CART to ride in. You must define, initiate, and revise as necessary: checkpoints, activities, relationships, and time estimates. As with the project goal and objectives, there is no express lane to the checkered flag. You must roll up your sleeves and dive into a process of thinking and analyzing, as precisely as you can, what needs to be done.

Checkpoints are like the markers that in ancient times were placed every so often along a road to let travelers know they were headed in the right direction. They served as visible reminders of progress. Checkpoints serve similar purposes in your race to the project finish line; they help you measure the progress of your project. There are both long-term and short-term checkpoints.

Milestones are the long-term checkpoints. They are used to measure actual versus planned progress on projects. They are visible and tangible measures of completion. They are significant events that tell you whether your project is on schedule, behind schedule, or ahead of schedule. If, for example, you are driving from Atlanta to Los Angeles, some of the major milestones might be Birmingham, Dallas, and Phoenix. Reaching these cities would indicate that you are getting closer to your final goal. Reaching them would also indicate whether you are still on course. Missing them would mean that you had to make adjustments. For example, if you found yourself in Chicago on your trip to Los Angeles, you would know you had made a wrong turn. But clearly you would like to know this before you got so far off track.

Events are the short-term checkpoints on your route to the goal. They are similar to milestones, but they occur more frequently, and thus there are more of them. Several events usually lead up to a particular milestone. Events provide feedback on a more regular, ongoing basis. They are useful at the operational level, whereas milestones provide more of an overview. On your trip from Atlanta to Los Angeles, some of the events might be getting onto Interstate 20 heading west out of Atlanta or reaching Meridian, Mississippi, a small town between Birmingham and Dallas. Events simply add further detail to the project course. They are shorter-term than milestones. Now, if in Atlanta you get on I-20 going east, you will know right away that you made a mistake and can correct it.

Checkpoints mark a specific instance in time, the accomplishment of something. What carries you from one event to the next, then to your milestones, and eventually to achieving project objectives and the project goal are *activities*. Activities are the tasks that must be completed in order to complete the project. In defining a project, you want to identify activities as precisely and in as much detail as possible. Don't overlook any activity necessary to complete the project, no matter how small. On your trip to Los Angeles, for example, failure to check your oil at a gas station stop could halt your entire project if the car runs too low on oil.

As Figure 3.1 illustrates, goals, objectives, checkpoints, and activities are highly interrelated and are crucial in any project journey. Thinking through the checkpoints and events and beginning to list activities will typically generate additional events and milestones that you did not think of at first. Defining checkpoints and activities is a back-and-forth process. But remember that you begin with the larger perspective of the goal and then become increasingly precise in looking at the objectives, then the milestones, then the events, and finally the required activities. You need to go from an overall picture down to the individual details. What you are doing is working backward from the goal of the project to the first step that you have to take to get to that goal. What is the first

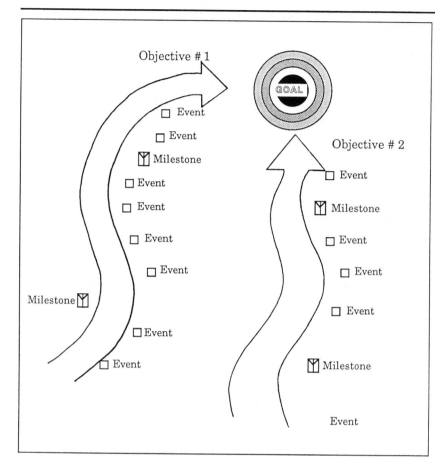

Figure 3.1

turn you take on your trip to Los Angeles? Which way do you go out of your driveway?

THE NOAH'S ARK PROJECT

Let us take another look at Noah's project of building and stocking the ark. What were some of the milestones, events, and activities?

Consider the carpenter's objective of building the ark according to specifications. This objective involves a complex process. Milestones and events add detail to the objective; they break it down into more manageable pieces. If Noah and the carpenters had had only the objective of completing the ark, all the thousands of additional things that were needed might never have been done, and the ark might never have been completed.

How did the milestones and events help Noah define his route and then monitor progress? Sample milestones might have been a completed layout of the ark, the skeleton of the ark built, and a male and female of each species in the waiting pen. Each milestone was a major event. By combining these with time estimates for the activities, Noah could know whether he was ahead of schedule, behind schedule, or on schedule. But had he known only that he needed to reach a milestone in a month, that might not have provided enough feedback to guide his direction and enable him to monitor his progress. He needed more specific direction.

The events provided that detail. Some of the events along the path to completing the ark's skeleton were putting the vertical supports on

Milestones	Events	Activities
Objectives for Noah's Ark Project Carpenters Put Ark Together		
I. One side of ark completed	1. Side supports built	a. Build vertical supports
	2. Sides completed	b. Build horizontal supports
	3. Railing built and mounted	c. Nail on slats
	4. Bottom support beam added	d. Paint leak filler on slats
		e. Build and mount railing
		f. Cut ramp opening
		g. Nail bottom support beam
II. Second side of ark completed	(Similar to above)	

Figure 3.2

each side in place, nailing on the side supports, and connecting the two sides. Noah could identify several events in the process of reaching the milestone of a completed skeleton, and those events gave him more detail. Listing the events also helped him define the actions he had to complete in building the ark. When he finished determining the events and activities, he had the beginnings of a route. Adding time estimates, he could know one week into this seven-month project that he needed to have the side layout completed. He knew that if he did not have this part of the layout, he was behind schedule. If he did have the layout, he was on schedule. As he defined the first step, the second step, and the third, he made the project more manageable. This is one of the primary advantages of having checkpoints and activities. They help to define exactly what you should be doing to get a project done. An activity is more manageable than a project. Figure 3.2 summarizes this information about the ark.

MONITORING AND MOTIVATION

Milestones and events also give you a useful way to plan and monitor progress on your project. You can continually check to determine if you are on schedule. Another valuable result that comes from having milestones, events, and activities is that they help to motivate people on the project.

Checkpoints serve as an essential form of feedback that helps project personnel stay committed and motivated. And they help monitor if the project is on schedule and within budget. Feedback has been called "the breakfast of champions." People thrive on it.

By giving your team members milestones and events, you set up a map for them so they can measure their location precisely. Remember the *M* in SMART goals and objectives. You want everybody on the project team to have a clear idea of what points on the map have to be passed in order to reach a certain destination. Without the map, people may stray from the road and not achieve their particular objective, let alone the project goal.

By giving people a well-conceived set of milestones and events, you provide them with a map to track their own progress and allow them to become excited about the project. They know what the project goal is—you've reminded them of it. They know what the objective is—you've clarified that. The checkpoints and activities provide points on the map that each individual can use as a tracking system to check progress. Each person knows that the objective is to reach Dallas by

Tuesday afternoon. If they pass Marshall, Texas, at noon, they know
that they are on schedule. People tend to get excited when they know
they are on track and making progress.

Milestones and events provide the map coordinates that help you
figure out the best route to your destination (the project objectives and
goal). They help you engage in contingency planning for when things
get off schedule. They provide a monitoring system to help you know
whether you are on or off schedule. They provide concrete feedback that
makes people feel responsible and accountable. People on the project
team have clear direction about where they are going, how they are being
tracked, and what they need to do along the way.

> Milestones and events
> help you monitor project
> progress. They also serve to
> motivate team members by
> providing feedback and
> direction!

Figure 3.3

Having milestones and events also gives you an opportunity to praise
progress and to recognize people's contributions. All too often, project
managers overlook these opportunities. By knowing precisely what the
schedule is and by being aware of it as people meet their checkpoints,
you can give them a pat on the back. This does wonders in terms of
energizing people and keeping them excited about the project. You don't
want to be like the bowling team captain who, when a teammate knocks
down seven of the ten pins on the first ball, yells, "You missed three."
Effective project managers use this opportunity to say, "Fantastic. You
knocked down seven. The three, five, and seven pins are left. Good luck
on the second ball." You are monitoring progress. You are giving feedback to people. And you are recognizing people's performance levels—
praising them for their contributions and solving problems with them
when they're behind schedule or not meeting expectations.

DETERMINING RELATIONSHIPS
AMONG THE ACTIVITIES

Once you have a complete list of the activities that make up a project,
you are ready for the next step—determining the *relationships* among
the activities. Certain activities may need to be performed before others,

but some activities can be performed simultaneously. You need to lay out the exact relationships among the activities. For example, on the ark, Noah had to build the frame before adding the side slats, but he could build the vertical supports at the same time as the horizontal supports (refer to Figure 3.2.).

The questions you ask are "What is the necessary order in which the activities must be done?" "What is the logical flow of activities?" and "What do technological requirements and resource availability dictate about the flow of activities?" Often you will find that there is more than one way to do the project. Determining the possible relationships among activities will help you identify efficient ways to get the job done and plan for unexpected contingencies. There is always more than one way to get the job done, and it is important to keep this in mind.

Getting the job done seldom depends on doing things in one *right way*. Perhaps two activities can be done in parallel rather than one after the other. Perhaps an activity one group was going to do can be done by another group. Try to anticipate the unexpected and consider ways to deal with it.

It is at this point that you address the "What if?" and "What could go wrong?" questions. What if this activity does not work out the way you think it will? What are some options if you encounter difficulties? Here you are engaged in contingency planning, a very important element in the project-planning process. Just be sure not to lose sight of the project goal.

ESTIMATING TIME AND OTHER RESOURCES

You also need to determine the amount of time, money, people, equipment, and other resources each activity will require. Such estimates allow you to plan the project more completely. Who needs to be involved in building the sides of Noah's ark? How long will it take? How much will it cost? Such decisions have to be made with limited information. Usually you do not know exactly how long a particular activity will take. You do not know exactly what resources will be needed. This is because each project is unique. The process of estimating resource requirements is especially challenging because you cannot predict the future and because things are likely to change once you implement the plan.

One estimation strategy that is useful when dealing with uncertain or unfamiliar activities requires coming up with three time estimates. The first estimate is an optimistic one—for example, the shortest possible time if everything falls into place. The second estimate is a pessimistic one—the time it will take if many things go wrong and you run into many difficulties. The third estimate is the most likely time—the time with the normal array of pluses and minuses. Such careful thinking helps you to further assess "what could go wrong" and what is really involved in completing an activity.

In making these three time estimates, it is also helpful to ask several members of the project team with relevant experience how long an activity will take. This information will help to refine your estimates. And as a side benefit, involving people in the estimation process builds their commitment to the eventual time estimate, encouraging the attitude "We told Noah we could find a male and female kangaroo in two days, and, by God, we'll do it!" Recognizing that all three are still estimates, you can calculate a weighted average to get a better idea of how long the activity will take. The equation for this is shown in Figure 3.4.

The time an activity will take will probably fall somewhere between the pessimistic and the optimistic times, and a precise estimate for the activity would be the expected time that comes out of the equation in Figure 3.4. This kind of calculation is not needed for every single activity in a project, but it is useful for critical activities with which you have little experience.

However, as a general principle it is always advisable to build extra resources (called slack) into your estimates. No one can predict the future with crystal ball certainty. Despite our best efforts at estimating, we almost always leave something out of the calculation or some unforeseen and unanticipated activity takes place. Slack is the grease effective project managers use when the project needs to be maneuvered back onto the track.

Whatever you do, the key is necessary spending the time and energy to come up with as good an estimate as possible for each of these activities. Otherwise, your GO-CART is likely to be way off track.

$$\text{Expected time} = \frac{\text{Optimistic time} + 4 \times \left(\text{Most Likely time} \right) + \text{Pessimistic time}}{\text{Divided by 6}}$$

Equation for Time Estimates

Figure 3.4

Objectives for Noah's Ark Project
Carpenters Put Ark Together

Milestones	Events	Activities	What activities must precede?	Time estimate	Who does it?
I. One side of ark completed	1. Side supports built	a. Build vertical supports		14 days	Noah's son Shem
	2. Sides completed	b. Build horizontal supports		10 days	Noah's son Ham
	3. Railing built and mounted	c. Nail on slats	a, b	14 days	Shem and Ham
	4. Bottom support beam added	d. Paint leak filler on slats	c	7 days	Noah's son Japheth
		e. Build and mount railing	b	2 days	Shem
		f. Cut ramp opening	e	1 day	Shem
		g. Nail bottom support beam	c	4 days	Ham and Sapheth
II. Second side of ark completed	(Similar to above)				

Figure 3.5

Even then, it is important to recognize that these times are *estimates*. Only after you have completed an activity will you really know how long it takes or how many other resources are needed. If you have done a similar project before, you may have a much better idea of how long it will take to complete an activity. But even then, the uniqueness of each project dictates that the resource figures you use are still estimates. Figure 3.5 on page 45 shows the Noah's ark time estimates, the activity relationships, and who is responsible for each activity. This figure shows the plan for one objective of the project.

CONCLUSION

The vehicle that will take you and your project to the finish line is a high-performance GO-CART. Building and assembling this vehicle takes time, discipline, and effort:

- Establish the project **G**oal
- Define project **O**bjectives
- Establish **C**heckpoints
- List the project **A**ctivities
- Determine **R**elationships among activities
- Make **T**ime estimates for activities

A systematic and, in some cases, arduous effort is required to get the job done. Putting the GO-CART together requires discipline. Skipping, eliminating, or short-circuiting these steps will lead to problems later on in the project.

Take a few moments to look over the ark project in Figure 3.5 again. Look at the milestones, events, activities, relationships, and time estimates. Now try thinking about one of the objectives on a project of yours. Create a list with milestones, events, activities, relationships, time estimates, and responsibilities. Then you too will have begun to build a GO-CART for your project.

The CART in GO-CART

Good Project Managers define:

- Checkpoints to mark project progress
- Activities that get the project done
- Relationships among the activities
- Time estimates for each activity

Figure 3.6

4

Rule Number Four
DRAW A PICTURE OF THE PROJECT SCHEDULE

Rule Number Four

DRAW A PICTURE OF THE PROJECT SCHEDULE

So far we have explored the essential, thorough, and rewarding process of planning your GO-CART. Unfortunately, many of us simply do not like to schedule, and that reduces our effectiveness. Studies show that successful people make the effort required to organize their time and activities. They make sure their behavior is in line with their goals. Doing the same with your projects will give you seven advantages:

1. You will have a *more realistic plan*—one that gives a more accurate picture of what will happen as your project progresses.
2. You will be better *able to anticipate* what needs to happen next.
3. You will know where to *concentrate your attention* to be sure the project stays on schedule and within the budget.
4. You will be able to *anticipate bottlenecks* and other coordination problems before they occur, so that you can take action to correct a delay before it becomes severe.
5. You will have a valuable tool to *enhance coordination and communication* among the project team members.
6. You will have a tool that helps to *build commitment*—because it publicly identifies responsibilities and deadlines and creates an awareness of inter-dependencies.
7. You will have a tool that leads to *completion* of projects *on time, within budget*, and *according to quality standards*.

But to make all of your planning most useful, you have to draw a picture of your GO-CART. You need to capture all of the information generated in the planning process in an easy-to-read and easy-to-use schedule. Since it is important that everyone knows about the type of the vehicle that will propel them to the finish line, we add an *S* to the end of GO-CART. The *S* stands for schedules. You need to draw two pictures. One is called a bar chart, the other a flow chart.

BAR CHARTS

Bar charts (also called Gantt charts) have proved their usefulness again and again. They are simple to draw, yet they capture a great amount of information about the project plan. They provide a useful overview of the project and constitute a quick management tool for monitoring project progress.

A bar chart has three basic parts: a time line, a list of activities, and a bar for each activity (the length of which represents the time estimated for the activity). A statement of the goal appears at the top of the page. Figure 4.1 shows a partial bar chart for Noah's ark.

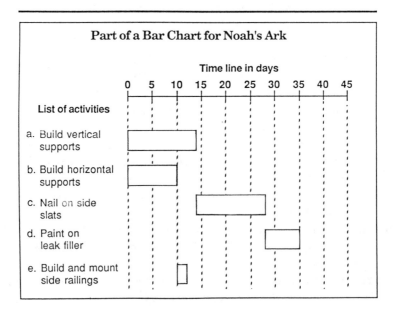

Figure 4.1

Bar charts provide an easy-to-read visual picture of activities, events, and milestones (the end points of bars mark completion of an activity). For example, "build vertical supports" is estimated to take 14 days, and "paint on leak filler" seven days. Bar charts also show the sequencing of activities—those that must be completed before others and those that can or must be done at the same time. In the bar chart for Noah's ark, "nail on side slats" must be done prior to "paint on leak filler," but "build vertical supports" and "build horizontal supports" can be done at the same time.

The familiar saying "A picture is worth a thousand words" is certainly true in the case of a bar chart. A bar chart can convey considerable information about a project very quickly. Typically, a bar chart is drawn on one page so that you can see an entire project and the accompanying set of activities at a glance. Since you can see the entire project, you also see a picture of the project goal.

A bar chart for an *entire project* typically collapses many activities together and shows only major events and milestones. To provide greater detail, you create a bar chart for each objective to define work for the various groups and individuals on the project team. For example, on the ark project, Noah's son Shem builds the vertical supports and the side railing and cuts the opening for the ramp. A bar chart of those activities helps him know what to do and when to do it. These additional bar charts help you coordinate the efforts of various groups working on different objectives. In this way you can begin to see the important interface points.

You can also use the bar chart to analyze "What if?" situations and determine the best plan for a project. It is easy to move the bars around on the chart to play with different options or to make contingency plans for "What could go wrong?" situations.

Furthermore, the bar chart can be used to track and monitor progress and to provide important feedback to team members. A common way of doing this is to shade in the bars to reflect percentage of completion for an activity.

Take a look again at the ark project (Figure 4.2). Point A on the time line reflects the current point in time. Combined with the shaded portion of the "build vertical supports" activity, you have an indication that the project is right on schedule. If the shaded portion extends to the right beyond point A, as it does for "build horizontal slats," it means you are ahead of schedule. If the shaded portion does not extend to point A, it means you are behind schedule. At a glance, you can tell where you are in relation to the schedule. If you are on or ahead of schedule, praise is called for; if you are behind, it is time for problem solving.

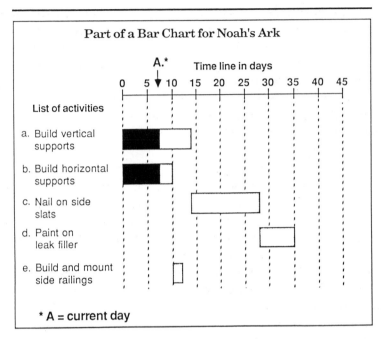

Figure 4.2

Since your bar chart allows you to spot problems early, it makes them easier to resolve.

You can also draw a bar chart to reflect the project budget, people requirements, equipment needs, and other resource allocations. Instead of listing activities in the left margin, you could put people's names, department names, or pieces of equipment. By using the bar chart that way, your planning can avoid overscheduling of people and equipment, especially among several projects. The bar chart can be used to track actual budget and other resource utilization versus planned utilization. Remember, you want projects done on time and according to desired quality standards, but also within a budget.

Keeping your bar chart up to date as the project proceeds and examining "What if?" questions can become somewhat tedious if you must continually redraw the bar chart. Fortunately, there are many excellent computer software programs to assist with this problem. Once you have your list of activities, their relationships, and the time estimates, you can enter these data into the computer and produce a bar chart. To update the chart, you simply feed in the new information. But don't get so hooked on the computer that you forget the project!

FLOW CHARTS

Another method for drawing a picture of a project schedule is the flow chart, also called a CPM (critical path method) or PERT (program evaluation and review technique) chart. Flow charts were developed in the early 1950s. They are somewhat more complex to draw than bar charts. They do not provide an easy view of the overall project and where you currently are on the project. But flow charts are extremely useful in identifying and managing the sequential flow of critical activities in a project. Like the bar chart, the flow chart has three basic components: arrows to represent activities, small circles to represent events and milestones, and written-in time estimates. Figure 4.3 illustrates a partial flow chart for Noah's ark (events are the hollow circles, milestones the shaded ones).

The flow of activities is readily apparent on a flow chart (hence their name). It is very clear, for example, that the vertical and horizontal supports must be completed on the ark before the side slats can be nailed on, whereas vertical and horizontal supports can be built at the same time. Also, all activities, events, milestones, and time estimates are easily accessible on the flow chart. Flow charts can be used to show the sequencing of activities for projects involving literally hundreds of activities.

One advantage of a flow chart over a bar chart is that the sequencing of every activity can be clearly displayed. Also, a flow chart more clearly shows interfaces with other activities. This feature is extremely valuable when two interfacing activities are done by two different people. Coordination can be greatly enhanced through this picture of the project sched-

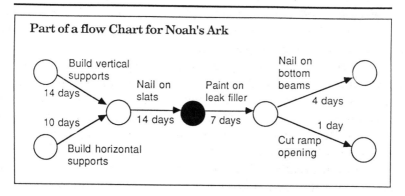

Part of a flow Chart for Noah's Ark

Build vertical supports — 14 days

Build horizontal supports — 10 days

Nail on slats — 14 days

Paint on leak filler — 7 days

Nail on bottom beams — 4 days

Cut ramp opening — 1 day

Figure 4.3

ule. Another advantage of a flow chart is that the longest sequence of activities in the project can easily be determined by adding up the time estimates along each path through the project. The longest path is called the "critical path" and determines the minimum amount of time for completing the project, since all paths must be completed before the project goal is achieved (see figure 4.4). The advantage of a flow chart is that a project with hundreds of activities can be coordinated. However, a flow chart with hundreds of activities is difficult to draw, so flow charts are usually drawn in sections and separated into time blocks. Computer software is also available for creating and manipulating flow charts, thus greatly simplifying their use.

WORKING WITH BAR AND FLOW CHARTS

For medium to large projects, both bar and flow charts are usually created. The flow charts aid in daily planning and execution of work on the project. The bar chart provides the overview that is used for coordinating and integrating individual objectives into the overall project goals and for monitoring budget and resource allocations. In building the ark, for example, Noah might have used a flow chart of the entire project and given pieces of it as bar charts to the carpenters, animal finders, food suppliers, and others. He might also have found a bar chart useful when talking to God to appraise him of the ark's progress. It is not at all uncommon to see project managers using both types of charts to maximize the strengths of both. And most computer software packages provide both types of charts as outputs from the same information input. These programs also allow you to budget and track resource use for each activity.

Like a bar chart, a flow chart can also be used to perform "What if?" analyses to determine the best plan for a project. Different charts can be drawn to represent alternative ways to complete the project. For each, the times along the paths can be added to determine the critical path. "What if?" analysis may enable you to figure out a way to get the project done more quickly than was originally thought possible. Denny's restaurants used these techniques to reduce significantly the project completion time on store conversion. The typical conversion cycle had been six months. But after purchasing 150 stores from other restaurant chains, Denny's knew they could not take that long for each conversion. By drawing pictures (bar and flow charts) of the conversion, they were able to play "What if?" games and reduce the time by one-third.

"What could go wrong?" analyses using a flow chart can help you

Partial Flow Chart for Noah's Ark

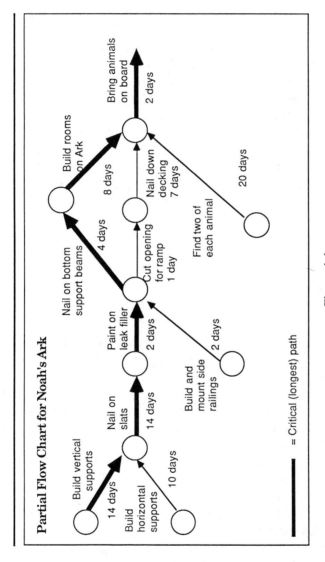

Figure 4.4

determine the impact on the project of a delay in any activity. You simply push the delay through the project to determine its impact. Often, delays will have minimal impact on overall project completion, because only delays on the longest path cause delays in project completion. Other paths have slack, since their total time estimates are less than that for the longest path.

How a flow chart can help in managing a project can be demonstrated by examining the abbreviated flow chart for Noah's ark (Figure 4.4). Of the seven possible paths on the flow chart, the one in bold arrows is the longest (44 days). This part of the project cannot be completed in less than 44 days. The other paths are shorter and hence have slack (extra time). For example, the side paths from "build horizontal supports" through "cut opening for ramps" are 36 days long. This means that delays of up to 8 days (44 − 36) can be tolerated on this path before the project completion date will be delayed.

As with the bar chart, you can update a flow chart regularly to reflect actual progress on the project. This is especially useful in determining changes in the estimate of overall project completion time and managing interfaces.

GETTING PROJECTS BACK ON TRACK

Flow charts and bar charts can also be quite useful in managing projects back on schedule when they fall behind. For example, slack on a particular path may indicate underutilized resources. Sometimes these resources can be shifted to the longest path to speed things along. In the Noah's ark chart (Figure 4.4), it is clear that there is slack on the "nail down decking" path. Perhaps these people could help build rooms on the ark if problems are encountered.

A related way to get projects back on track is to shift slack time. Consider using the slack at the beginning, in the middle, or at the end of an activity. Noah, for example, could find the animals early in the project and hold them in a pen. Meanwhile, some of the animal finders could help on other paths of the project.

Of course, you can allocate overtime, add shifts, or bring in sub-contractors to help get projects back on schedule, but you must monitor costs to keep them under control. The key here is to use your flow charts and bar charts to help you consider alternatives. There is always more than one way to complete a project. By being creative and conducting "What if we did it this way?" discussions, you can use the bar charts and flow charts to help get the project done on time, within budget, and according to quality standards.

A NOTE ON COMPUTER SOFTWARE

As you might imagine, the planning, modification, contingency planning, and updating for complicated projects is much easier if you can use a project management software package on a computer. But it is important to recognize that a computer cannot do the steps outlined in Rules One, Two, or Three. It cannot set goals or objectives, nor can it define checkpoints, activities, relationships, and time estimates. The project manager and team must do these things before the computer can aid in drawing a picture of the schedule. And for simple projects, resorting to the computer is probably not worth the trouble.

Once you decide that a computer software package would be useful on your personal computer (which is what most project managers use), you embark on the project of selecting the right package from among the several hundred available on the market today. To select effectively, you first need to know what you want the software to do. For example, do you want bar chart and flow chart capabilities? What types of output reports do you want? Do you want the package to handle resource and budget allocations? Do you want it to put things on a calendar for you? Is the software user-friendly? Do the software manufacturer and distributor have good reputations?

Second, you should be sure that the software package can perform at least the following functions:

1. Permits easy development and changes in project bar charts and flow charts and notes the critical path.
2. Allows you to see a bar chart or flow chart on the computer screen before printing it. And the charts are easy to follow on the screen.
3. Permits you to combine resource and budget information into the project file and to retrieve useful reports on this information.
4. Allows you to tie your project plan to a real calendar, with allowances for weekends and holidays.
5. Alerts you to overscheduling of individuals or groups, as well as to errors in the logic of your dependencies on the flow chart.
6. Allows you to construct "What if?" scenarios so that you can engage in contingency planning and update modifications.
7. Has a good demonstration file to show you what the program can do; also has a user-friendly user's manual.

Third, experiment with the package on a project you have already completed. Let the package convince you that it could have helped. Above all, remember that the computer software, with its reports and files, is only a tool to help you manage the project. The computer will not manage it for you. That is your job.

CONCLUSION

So, there you have it, two ways—bar charts and flow charts—to draw a picture of a project schedule. Two ways that summarize all the planning we discussed in the first three rules. By following the planning process, your project plan will move more smoothly through the implementation phase and toward successful completion.

Drawing these pictures gets easier with practice. Try drawing one for a project that you are working on now.

The S in GO-CARTS

To make your GO-CART plan the most useful, you have to draw a picture of the Schedule.

Figure 4.5

Having good equipment, like a GO-CART, is necessary for getting the job done, but it's not enough. The plan and schedule are not the end objectives of the project, only the means. We still need a DRIVER. Someone still has to drive this vehicle to the finish line—sometimes over rough terrain, through rush-hour traffic, over forgotten back roads and modern expressways. The skills and perspectives required to do this successfully make up the next six rules.

5

Rule Number Five

DIRECT PEOPLE INDIVIDUALLY AND AS A PROJECT TEAM

DIRECT PEOPLE INDIVIDUALLY AND AS A PROJECT TEAM

The most basic, fundamental, and often overlooked rule about success-fully managing projects is *You can't do it alone!* Time and again studies reveal that projects fail because the project manager has not built a strong team of supporters and collaborators. This generally happens because of the project manager's insensitivity to other people. This unwillingness, or inability, to understand the perspective of others has been diagnosed as the primary reason managers are not successful in their careers.

There is no easy formula for managing people on project teams. Ultimately our management strategies are based on an understanding of people and of what makes them tick. Indeed, we all know something about people. And we all have theories about why people do what they do. To be a successful project manager, you cannot be limited by your personal experience and commonsense knowledge of human behavior. Most important, you need to know how to put yourself in the other person's shoes. To manage the members of your project team, you must understand the fundamental nature of human behavior and appreciate other people's motivations. This information will increase your awareness of your own motivation. As Noah learned about himself and his own needs and values, he also learned how to build a strong project team. And without the team he could never have completed the ark on time—and we would all be history!

KNOW THYSELF

Where you begin in understanding what makes someone else tick is by understanding yourself. Noah's commitment to God was tested and challenged, and ultimately strengthened, by God's request of him to lead the ark project. One way to understand more about yourself is to reflect on your past experiences. Where have you been victorious? What contributed to your success? How did you feel? Where have been your disappointments? What would you do differently? Can you articulate the lessons from your life, from the peaks as well as the valleys?

Studies reveal that people learn best about being (and becoming) effective managers by deriving lessons from their experiences. For example, when you complete a project, time and energy should be devoted to the questions "What did we learn?" "How could we have accomplished this better?" and "What will we do similarly or differently next time?" Doing this leads to an accumulation of experiential learnings, rather than ten years of experience being the result of one year's experience repeated ten times.

Know thyself and
you will begin to
understand others.

Figure 5.1

Another important reason for self-awareness is that our expectations about other people create blinders that cause us to limit our appreciation of others. In many instances we see what we expect to see rather than what is actually occurring. Expectations are powerful—they form frames into which we fit others' behavior. If we believe that some people on the project are lazy, we will interpret their behavior as lazy. Only behavior that is clearly contrary to our expectations will cause us to change the way we see things. And even then we are likely to be unhappy about changing because it means we have to admit that we made a mistake!

Expectations also influence our attitudes and behavior toward other people. This tendency has been called a "self-fulfilling prophecy." When we behave toward others according to the way we expect them to respond (for example, closely supervising those we predict will be lazy), they often will act as we expect—because of *our* behavior. In effect, our actions create the situation we expect, thus reinforcing our initial perception.

As social psychologist Douglas McGregor observed, "Managers are prisoners of their own assumptions about human nature." His propositions about "Theory X" (where employees are viewed as lazy and irresponsible) versus "Theory Y" (where employees are viewed as responsible and hardworking) show how managers' assumptions about people determine their managerial strategies. These assumptions in turn influence the way their subordinates work. Psychologists have found that rats identified to their handlers as "maze-bright" run mazes more quickly than rats introduced to their handlers as being "dumb"; students identified to their teachers as "intellectual bloomers" do better on achievement tests than students who lack such a positive introduction; and job trainees pointed out to their supervisors as having "special potential" perform better than trainees not so identified. In all cases, there is no real difference between the two groups, only a difference in the superior's expectations.

It is important to know ourselves and our expectations before trying to know about someone else, especially if we hope to motivate the people on our project team. Many theories of motivation have been developed. Your success in motivating others is likely to result from thinking through the implications of your responses to these two questions:

1. Have you ever done anything in your life that was stupid?
2. Have you ever met an unmotivated person?

Would you say yes or no to these questions?

IT MAKES SENSE TO ME

Have you ever done anything in your life that was stupid? Most of us would have to say yes (at least once). But when we reflect on that foolish behavior, did we act that way because we wanted to be stupid or foolish? Certainly not. To understand another person's behavior, we need to see it from that person's point of view. We need to ask the question "How does this behavior make sense to that person?" By using this perspective, we can be analytical and descriptive about what people are doing rather than evaluative and general.

Remember that your perception of reality is not always the same as someone else's. For example, it seems stupid to you that engineering has not released the design plans, even though they are completed and already two months past due. But it makes sense to the engineers because they believe that their appeal for additional staff will be stronger if it appears that they need more personnel (that is, that it takes so long to complete design plans). Or consider how it makes perfect sense and seems only fair to me when I leave the office a few hours early on Friday. After all, I'll be back in again on Saturday, and the company "owes" me some time off with my family. But to my boss, this behavior appears wrong because my departure suggests a lack of real commitment to the project. Just imagine God saying to Noah, "Noah, what are you doing getting the animals together before the ark is completed? Are you crazy?" And Noah saying, "Wait a minute, what I'm trying to do is . . ." Each side needs to understand the perspective of the other.

ALL PEOPLE ARE MOTIVATED

Have you ever met an unmotivated person? Most of us agree that we have. But this is a trick question. If it's true, individual behavior would be random and capricious—and behavior is neither. As we discussed, all actions make sense to the people doing the acting. When we respond affirmatively to this question, what we're thinking about is a person who is motivated to do something other than what we want that person to be doing. All people are motivated. The questions is, "Motivated to do what?" Consequently, it is from our perspective, and not theirs, that they are *not* motivated. As a project manager, you might think about motivation as the area of overlap between project goals and individual goals.

> All people are motivated;
> the question is
>
> *"Motivated to do what?"*

Figure 5.2

All behavior is directed toward the satisfaction of individual needs. Find out more about the needs, desires, wants, and goals of the members of your project team, and you have some chance of motivating their behavior—assuming that you can help them satisfy their needs.

Knowing a person's needs is crucial because needs that are already satisfied do not motivate or influence people's behavior. It is difficult, for example, to motivate state-of-the-art engineers by threatening to fire them when they can easily go out and find another job. Furthermore, people do not focus on higher-level needs when their lower-level needs are not being met. For instance, it would be hard to encourage more innovation from a marketing group whose members are worried about whether they are going to lose their jobs, be relocated, or phased out.

PEOPLE ARE DIFFERENT AND INCONSISTENT

The basic dilemma in working with people lies in this paradox: People are alike and people are different. Although this proposition is obviously true, the way it translates into behavior is often very subtle. Maintaining a balance between treating everyone the same (or managing everyone consistently) and being sensitive to individual differences is not easy. Striving to attain such harmony is at the heart of Hewlett-Packard's famous "HP Way." Hewlett-Packard managers are expected to treat individuals with respect and dignity while coordinating their activities with consistency and continuity.

We are all alike in that we share biological needs for food, shelter, air, and water. We differ, however, in our preferences for the flavor, texture, quantity, or quality of nourishment. We are alike in that we share basic psychological needs for belonging, love, acceptance, and accomplishment. But we differ in the degree to which we want to be included or want to include others and in our ability to love and to be affectionate. We are physiologically alike in that we have two eyes, two ears, a nose, a mouth, and a mind. However, we differ in appearance, physical condition, and mental ability. Everyone has interests, goals, and a personality, but everyone's interests, goals, and personality are unique. As a project manager, you face the challenge of balancing consistency and equity in relating to people. Dealing with the different personalities on a project team requires considerable skill and often much ingenuity. Remember, there is nothing so unequal as the equal treatment of unequals.

In addition, the challenge of motivating the efforts of the people on your project team is complicated because no one ever behaves consistently—probably because no two situations are ever exactly alike. An understanding of the perceptual process helps to explain this. Simply put, we behave in terms of our perception of reality, and that perception is

> There is nothing so unequal as the equal treatment of unequals.

Figure 5.3

determined partly by what's outside of us and partly by what's inside of us.

The physiological aspect of perception defines the limit of what we can actually see, hear, smell, or feel. Yet even given these limitations, the information gathered by our senses does not enter our minds as raw or unprocessed data. Each person's perception or window on the world is shaped and bounded by upbringing and family experiences, education and training, and cultural values. We tend to interpret information in a way that is consistent with our beliefs, values, and attitudes, which are shaped by larger cultural and environmental experiences. Our perception is determined by the interaction between physiological and psychological factors.

Perceptual differences can readily influence the ways in which project personnel respond to organizational and managerial practices. Different individuals, for example, vary in terms of the importance they attach to job-related rewards, the style of leadership they prefer, their need for interpersonal contact and interaction, and their tolerance and acceptance of job responsibility. Could Noah treat everyone working on the ark the same way? Not if he expected to get it done on time. Different people must be treated differently.

The implications for you as a project manager are clear. Don't expect other people to view things exactly as you do, no matter how clear things seem to you and how certain you are about the accuracy of your point of view. Expect differences since each person filters the same information through a different screen.

CONCLUSION

Effective project managers know that while individuals may win trophies, it is teamwork that brings championships. John Wooden, the most successful college basketball coach of all time, tells his secret: "I never told the players to go out and win. I told them to go out and play so that after the game they could look at themselves in the mirror and say that they did everything possible to be their best that day." Applying this mirror test to our project team requires being aware of our expectations and assumptions, attempting to understand the other person's perspective and hence their needs, and respecting each individual's uniqueness. Project managers who are sensitive to why people do what they do are a step ahead of their colleagues when it comes to directing the efforts of the project team toward the finish line.

Figure 5.4

> Tell your people to "go out and
> play so . . . they can look themselves
> in the mirror and say that they
> did everything possible to be
> their best . . ."

6

Rule Number Six

REINFORCE
THE COMMITMENT
AND EXCITEMENT
OF THE PROJECT TEAM

Rule Number Six

REINFORCE THE COMMITMENT
AND EXCITEMENT OF THE PROJECT TEAM

Several years ago a special project group at Data General was assigned the task of designing a new computer. The project manager used special rituals to get people excited and committed to the project. For example, every member of the project team passed through an initiation rite called signing up. By signing up for the project, a person agreed to do whatever was necessary to make the project succeed. This could mean forsaking family, friends, hobbies, and all vestiges of a nonwork life until the project was completed.

The reasons behind this signing-up ritual were simple. People who make this kind of commitment to a project no longer need to be coerced to work on it. They have volunteered. Indeed, an internal study by Texas Instruments found that the best predictor of project success was whether the project participants had volunteered for the project.

Data General went to great lengths to get an unusually high degree of commitment to the computer design project; you will not always need this kind of commitment to a job. You will, however, need to make sure that your project team is behind the project, working in the same direction to achieve the project's goals, rather than in front of the project, acting as roadblocks to progress. To accomplish this, you need to do more than lay out the project goals and objectives and issue instructions about what to do. You need to make team members feel that they are participating in an exciting venture, guided by a shared vision of how their efforts will bring success. Imagine the initial project meetings between Noah and his team. Noah says, "OK, who wants to help build the ark?"

Laughter follows. "Noah, you must be kidding," replies one person. Another says, "Noah, there's not going to be a flood. Be serious."

"But God told me . . ."

More laughter. Sometimes it can be a challenge to build commitment and excitement around a project.

> You want your project team
> **behind** the project, rather than
> **in front** acting as roadblocks.

Figure 6.1

BUILDING COMMITMENT

Researchers have demonstrated how companies build strong organizational cultures, maintaining high levels of commitment and loyalty. Basic to this process is what Tom Peters and Bob Waterman articulated in their best-selling book about America's excellent companies, *In Search of Excellence*: "Figure out your value system. Decide what your company stands for."

Excellent companies and high-performing project teams have clearly articulated values about how they intend to run their businesses or projects. This clarity creates a shared belief among people that focusing and adhering to these values will bring them success. Research has shown that commitment, loyalty, and pride, as well as organizational productivity, are directly related to the clarity, consensus, and intensity of organizational values and standards. Correspondence between personal and organizational values significantly affects levels of individual commitment, willingness to work hard, attachment to customers, and levels of job satisfaction and effectiveness.

Making full use of the intelligence of project members is essential to the success of any enterprise. The recent emphasis on quality circles and total quality control programs at such companies as Hewlett-Packard, Schlumberger, Memorex, Hughes Aircraft, Polaroid, and Signetics stems from the recognition that employees at all levels have good ideas about how to improve productivity, and managers can benefit by using them.

Consider the experience of IBM. The independent task force responsible for what was to become the company's highly successful personal computer was established as an independent business unit. It was not subject to the same rules that required most IBM product design teams to account for their every move. As one of the PC designers put it: "If you're going to compete with five men in a garage, you have to do something different." What IBM did differently was grant the team considerable autonomy to make its own decisions, as if it were a small business itself rather than submerged in a larger company.

IBM was granting its managers the freedom to make full use of the intelligence and capability of the people involved in this project. It placed relatively few constraints on the decisions the project team could make. IBM gave the team fairly broad goals but little further direction on how to achieve them.

As another example, Lockheed Corporation has credited nearly $3 million in savings to its productivity improvement program from small task groups. And Honeywell used the intelligence of one of its quality circles to reduce the cost of an electronics product by nearly 20 percent and won a government contract sought by a number of its competitors.

In short, project teams achieve the best results when members have the chance to contribute their own ideas to the project and to share responsibility for making important decisions. These conditions give project team members the opportunity to experience their work as meaningful. Surveys show that this is a critical motivator for professionals today.

To build commitment to the project, instill company values and let people contribute their ideas on how to succeed.

Figure 6.2

BUILDING EXCITEMENT

You must also provide opportunities to "encourage the heart" of the members of your project team. Some project managers make the mistake of assuming that individuals respond only to money. Although increases in salary or bonuses are certainly appreciated, people's preferences for rewards extend much further. Verbal recognition of performance in front of one's peers and visible awards, such as certificates, plaques, and other tangible gifts, are powerful rewards.

One senior bank officer placed a large bell in the middle of the office. Every time someone made a loan, he or she got to ring it. At Mervyn's Department Stores, top executives send out note cards that have "I heard something good about you" printed at the top. They send them not just to other officers but also to clerks, buyers, trainees, and other line employees. After every ball game during its 1983 season, the Los Angeles Dodgers baseball team gave a "Mr. Potato Head" award to the best performer. The award lightened the clubhouse atmosphere and rewarded good performance as well. Many people believe it contributed to the team's winning of its division that year. "Sticker redemption nights" are held monthly in one large manufacturing company. At this time, employees can redeem the stickers received for extra effort during the month for food and beverages.

Such ceremonies may border on the silly. However, they provide a healthy opportunity for people to recognize their success and to celebrate that success with others. More important, they encourage shared visions of success far more than monetary rewards can. At North American Tool and Die Company, the "Super Person of the Month" award is given to the person most responsible for helping the company achieve its goal of "no rejects." You should always be on the lookout for ways to spread the psychological benefits of making people feel like winners. Winners contribute in important ways to the success of their projects, and most people on the project team can be winners, given the chance.

GETTING PEOPLE COMMITTED AND EXCITED

There are many ways to get people on your project committed and excited. Here are five of the most successful:

1. Create challenging possibilities.
2. Inspire a shared vision.
3. Increase visibility.
4. Empower people.
5. Spread the "attaboys" around.

1. *Create challenging possibilities* by giving people the big picture and by promoting the meaningfulness of their efforts. Make sure everyone

on the project knows the overall project goal. "We're trying to build an ark that will save us from the flood. Don't lose sight of how each board you nail on is part of the ark." Your people need to know at the outset not only what they are trying to accomplish but for whom and why. To do otherwise is to foster the alienation and apathy of "it's just another job!" Tandem Computers goes to considerable efforts to give every one of its employees an understanding of the company's business and five-year plan. Every employee attends a two-day seminar on this subject. Letting people see the big picture and peek at strategic secrets boosts commitment and energy.

2. *Inspire a shared vision* of the project's purpose and goal. Bob Swiggett, chairman of Kollmorgen Corporation, straightforwardly remarks: "The leader's job is to create a vision." Henry Boettinger, former director of corporate planning with AT&T, says prophetically, "If a manager loses heart and does not follow any dream or vision, the organization is doomed." Noah was able to transmit his faith to others, so that together they were able to persist in the ark project, even when it appeared foolish to people around them. Your clarity of focus and perspective foster inspiration; after all, you can't light a fire with a wet match! When goals are shared by project team members, they are more likely to be committed, loyal, productive, willing to put in long hours, and much less hassled and tense. Evidence of this dedication is the T-shirt worn by members of Apple Computer's product development group: "Working 90 hours a week and loving it."

> You can't light a fire
> with a wet match!

Figure 6.3

3. *Increase visibility* of the project team's efforts. Part of the magic behind schedules (bar charts and flow charts) is that they are public. They make visible the commitments of each member of the project. They make people accountable and provide ongoing feedback about results. They also provide information about critical interdependencies. Without a sense of interdependency, team members will feel little incentive to cooperate with others or to feel a shared sense of responsibility and fate. Visibility may be the psychological glue that holds most religions together. Congregants are constantly demonstrating their beliefs together with their peers publicly. You need to "get religion" for your team by making

project team members' efforts visible for one another. At companies like Action Instruments and ShareData employees are expected to take an active interest in the company's management and success. An "info center" supplies workers with the detailed information usually given only to top managers at many companies. Everybody knows what everyone else is doing and is supposed to be doing. Hence everyone can help one another out; everyone can cooperate more effectively.

4. *Empower people* to be effective by using their intelligence and natural drive. Empowering others means giving them the resources and authority necessary to make things happen. Give your project team the chance to perform. Give them the data, the goals, and the freedom to operate. Successful managers know that giving away power in this fashion does not reduce their own power. On the contrary, as one hospital administrator exclaimed: "Since I've started being more participative—giving power away—I've never had so much authority." This premise has been well tested. Effective project managers find that empowering others—sharing their power and responsibility—results in more committed and more responsible project participants. Putting power in the hands of others is like investing money in a certificate of deposit: It is guaranteed to pay high interest.

5. *Spread the "attaboys" around* is another successful investment strategy. Project team members seldom complain that they are thanked too much by their managers. Among the many purposes that milestones serve should be marking times for celebration. People want to be effective, they want to be noticed, and they want to be appreciated. Successful project managers understand that people just want to be winners. People don't begin each day with a desire to lose. It is part of your job to show

---

People don't start each day with a desire to lose. Help them win by:

• Creating exciting possibilities

• Inspiring a shared vision

• Increasing visibility

• Empowerment

• Spreading "attaboys" around

Figure 6.4

people that they can win. A key characteristic of excellent companies is the exuberance with which they celebrate accomplishments. Spreading the good word about the accomplishments of your people will increase their visibility and enhance their own power and reputation. Some of the credit will inevitably find its way back to you. Your ability to get people excited and committed will get noticed.

CONCLUSION

Reinforcing the commitment and excitement of the project team means motivating them. And motivation is tricky. You don't really motivate others. Rather, you allow people's motivation to be directed toward project goals. The unfortunate truth is that the average project member uses only 30 percent of his or her potential. By following the ideas given here, you can begin to tap in to the other 70 percent. The payoff can be quite large. People will work just as hard when you are not around as when you are. Your ark will get done on time and within budget.

7

Rule Number Seven

KEEP EVERYONE CONNECTED WITH THE PROJECT INFORMED

Rule Number Seven

KEEP EVERYONE CONNECTED
WITH THE PROJECT INFORMED

Most project managers do not communicate as effectively as they should. They do not keep people on the project team, upper management, or themselves properly informed. Communication problems are experienced more often than anyone would like to admit. Have you ever experienced the kind of communication problem depicted in Figure 7.1 on page 84? Many of us do all too often. But stop for a minute and think about why.

BARRIERS TO EFFECTIVE INFORMATION FLOW

If you think about it, you can probably come up with quite a list of reasons why communication problems exist. Most of these reasons fall into two categories of barriers: personal and organizational. Personal barriers include such things as emotions, preoccupation, hostility, past experiences, hidden agendas, inarticulateness, stereotyping, physical environment (like machine noise and telephone interruptions), daydreaming, defensiveness, and information overload.

For example, Noah's woodcutters might say, "Those carpenters wouldn't know a good board if they saw one. They're all stupid" (stereotyping). Or the thunder is crackling as they try to finish the ark. Noah says, "God, I can't hear you" (noise). Unfortunately, project team members often place greater emphasis on these personal barriers than they should. How many times have you heard "We just have a personality

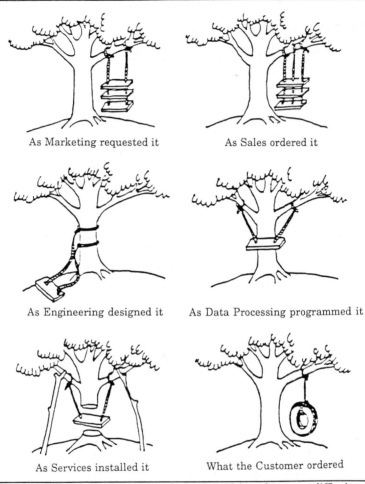

As Marketing requested it   As Sales ordered it

As Engineering designed it   As Data Processing programmed it

As Services installed it   What the Customer ordered

Communication breakdowns make meaningful performance difficult.

Figure 7.1   (From *Let's Talk*, 2nd ed. by Sathre, Olson, and Whitney. Copyright © 1977, 1973 by Scott, Foresman and Company. Reprinted by permission.)

conflict,'' as though there were no hope for solution short of eliminating one or both of the team members.

Often organizational barriers are much more important in communication problems on projects. This is because of the very nature of a project. Projects involve people from different departments, who use different languages, have different objectives, have had different types of training, and yet must work together closely on a unique task. Typical organizational barriers to communications include an organizational structure that separates the departments, special languages and jargon, status differences among departments, information overload or sometimes underload (too little information), ambiguity leading to incomplete information or faulty transmission of information, and time pressures.

For example, Noah's woodcutters cannot communicate with his animal handlers because of language differences. The trunks of animals are quite different from the trunks of trees, yet the words are the same. Kiln-dried wood, though of critical importance to woodcutters, may not mean anything to the animal handlers. And aren't the animal selectors the most important players on the team? Just ask them.

You could add several more barriers to either list, but the real issue is what you can do to overcome these barriers. What do you need to do to get your message across more effectively? What do you need to do to be a better listener? The answers are deceptively simple; the trick is having the discipline to use the answers.

HOW YOU CAN GET YOUR MESSAGE ACROSS

As the sender of a message, the knack is to get the other person to listen to what you are saying. Four basic practices can help you as the sender to improve communication:

1. Hit others where they are.
2. Make certain the receiver knows why your message is important.
3. Keep the other person posted.
4. Communicate assertively.

1. *Hit others where they are.* Know what is on other people's minds. What needs or problems are they thinking about? What words, phrases, or analogies will make the most sense to them? Often, you know what you want to say. However, it is not as important that your message be clear to you as it is that it be clear to the person you want to receive your message. Basically, this is a marketing concept. It means that you must package your ideas in ways that make it easy for others to tune in to you. This does not mean that you have to change your idea, simply its presentation.

An example from the advertising world will make this point clear. A television commercial for a toothpaste presents two attractive people of the opposite sex. What is the advertiser trying to sell you? Toothpaste, fewer cavities, or better interpersonal relations? What the advertiser is telling you is that you too will have greater sex appeal if you use this particular brand. And the young adult market hears the message loud and clear.

But what if the intended audience is children? Do the advertisers use the same sex appeal approach? "Use our toothpaste and be the sexiest 5-year-old on the block"? Of course not. They focus in on tasting good and fighting cavities because the audience is really the parents of 5-year-olds. But the contents of the two brands are almost identical. They are just packaged and marketed differently in order to "hit others where they are." It works. Try it and you will see. But remember that it all starts with being sensitive to the needs of the person on the receiving end of your message.

2. *Make certain the receiver knows why your message is important.* People perceive the world around them in their own terms. Their terms and your terms may not be the same. Therefore, you need to understand the interests and needs of the person with whom you are communicating. The best way to get their attention is through what people in marketing refer to as "benefits selling." Consider the following example.

Burt Hinson is a very successful salesperson for a large insurance company. He has made contact with a potential new client, Jim Steward. They are meeting at Jim's house tonight to discuss Jim's life insurance program. After a brief casual conversation, Burt gets to the point.

"Jim, let me ask you a few questions."

"All right," says Jim.

"Jim, do you have all the money that you really need in your life?" says Burt.

Very matter-of-factly, Jim replies, "No, of course I don't."

"OK," says Burt. "Let me ask you another question. If you were to die tomorrow, would your family have enough money for the mortgage, for living expenses, for college for your lovely kids?"

Jim hesitates, and Burt quickly holds up his hand and says, "That's OK, Jim, I understand. But let me ask you just one more question, Jim. Do you love your family?"

Gulp! Now Jim has a problem he did not have a few minutes ago. He is motivated to listen to Burt as they discuss ways to match Jim's love for his family and his financial resources. Burt is in a position to "help Jim solve his problems."

Of course, this example is a little extreme, but it makes the point. You have probably had something not too different from this happen to you. Burt has told Jim "why he should listen" and has "made it clear how his message can help him."

3. *Keeping the other person posted.* You can be a better communicator if you keep information flowing on a regular basis. One of the biggest mistakes many project managers make is not communicating with project team members in a consistent, ongoing fashion. Furthermore, they do not communicate regularly with upper management and then seem surprised when management keeps asking what is going on. All things considered, no one really likes surprises—neither your boss nor your project team.

Remember, good project performance is not just the final goal; it is all the steps it takes to get from start to finish. Constantly monitoring progress, along with regular feedback to project team members, is the key to avoiding many communication problems. Likewise, keeping your boss or bosses informed helps to minimize the likelihood of having the rug pulled out from under you in the eleventh hour. Not surprising top management means that your requests to them will tend to be of a smaller incremental nature. Small incremental requests have a higher probability of being granted than resource requests to solve big problems.

4. *Communicate assertively with understanding.* Do you communicate assertively? Or aggressively? Many project managers do not understand the difference. They think that communicating assertively means making sure that they get their point across and have it acted on. But that kind of communication is really aggressive.

Figure 7.2 illustrates the difference between assertive, aggressive, and submissive communications. When you are aggressive, you promote

Aggressive, Assertive, Submissive Framework

	Your ideas	Other's ideas
Aggressive	Used	Lost
Assertive	Heard	Heard
Submissive	Lost	Used

Figure 7.2

only your ideas and try to exclude the other person's ideas. If you have the bigger club, you will probably win, at least in the short run. When you are submissive, your ideas are the ones that get lost. The other person's ideas will be adopted, assuming that he or she is also not submissive. When you are assertive, you try to be sure that your ideas are heard, but you also try to listen to the other person's ideas. The result is true communication and better problem solving because both people get their ideas out on the table and attended to.

There are four possible outcomes when two people communicate assertively: (1) Your ideas get used, (2) the other person's ideas get used, (3) a compromise of ideas gets used, and (4) the really exciting possibility—a completely new set of ideas that neither of you had thought of—emerges and gets used. Two heads really are better than one.

The key to assertive communication is the concept of understanding. Being understanding means that you actively focus on making sense of the other person's ideas. If the person is quiet and does not volunteer thoughts, you need to draw out the person's original ideas and reactions to your ideas. If the other person is submissive, your focus will need to be almost entirely on understanding and very little on assertiveness. If the person is aggressive, your focus may shift more toward assertiveness, although understanding can also help calm down the other person. Two assertive people tend to use a relatively equal blend of assertiveness and understanding. The primary point is that by blending assertiveness and understanding, you will be focusing on the message going from sender to receiver and on the feedback going from receiver to sender. This can only improve the level of communication on a project. See figure 7.4 on page 91.

HOW YOU CAN BECOME A BETTER LISTENER

Most project managers are not very good listeners. Yet almost 45 percent of the time spent in managing projects is spent in receiving information. Listening is often a badly managed skill. Tests of listening comprehension show that we typically hear only about 25 percent of the information that comes to us. You can become a much better listener if you discipline yourself to use the following eight suggestions.

1. *Be prepared to listen.* Hear what the other person is trying to tell you. You have to want to hear the message coming to you. You need to scan constantly for messages. Sometimes they come very directly and clearly; at other times they are almost imperceptible. Being prepared also

means cutting down on the distractions (for example, the telephone ringing).

2. *Stop talking.* No good ideas ever entered the head through an open mouth! Some project managers try to get things done faster by talking more and listening less. But research has shown that the best project managers learn as much as possible about what is going on by listening carefully to others.

STOP TALKING

... No good idea ever entered
the head through an open mouth.

Figure 7.3

3. *Listen with understanding.* Put yourself in the other person's position so that you can better appreciate the language and focus on the message. If the message is unclear, you may need to use your understanding/assertive approach to clarify the message. If the project team member is very angry, you may need to hear and acknowledge the anger before you can get to the real message. Remember, your primary objective when listening is to understand clearly the message being sent.

4. *Hear the speaker out completely.* Be sure you have heard the other person before you begin sending messages back. This does not mean that you cannot ask questions to clarify the message or paraphrase the message to check your interpretation. But be sure you do not cut off the person talking. Have you ever had someone complete a sentence for you? More often than not, such pests complete it incorrectly. Then you must erase their mistake and try again to get your idea through to them.

5. *Listen for what is not said.* For example, you say to one of the team members, ''Sharon, would you please check the files on the shelf-life studies and summarize the results in a memo by this Friday?'' Sharon responds, ''Sure, I'll look into it.'' Sound OK? You could easily assume that Sharon will get the job done by Friday. But wait a minute. What did Sharon *not* say? She did not say that she would prepare the memo. A little more time on the issue and checking to ensure clear communication might help avoid a disappointment for both of you on Friday.

6. *Listen for how something is said.* Pay attention to the feelings or emotional level of the message. Notice eye contact, gestures, body language, tone of voice, timing, and other nonverbal signals. Over 70

percent of our interpersonal communication is nonverbal; only 30 percent of the message is in the words we use. Imagine trying to convince a department manager to redo something the employees have already completed. The manager says, "I am open to discussing it." But sits behind the desk, leans back in the chair, crosses his/her arms, and waits for you to make the first move. How open is this person?

Or imagine a project team meeting where two of the team members have positioned themselves out of the circle. Two other people continue to survey the floor and the ceiling with their eyes. Only you and one other team member seem to be discussing working late on New Year's Eve. What do you think is going to happen when it comes time to work hard and late on December 31? The nonverbal messages suggest that you may encounter some problems.

7. *Wait out pauses*. Give the project team member who has an idea the time to share it with you fully. Wait for that department manager to collect her thoughts before she responds to your request for four of her people to work a greater percentage of their time on your project. You want people's true response, so be patient. When you are silent, you invite others to fill the air with the sound of their voice. Patience is a virtue.

8. *Provide feedback*. Let others know what you heard and what you are going to do with their request, order, or information. Your primary responsibility as a listener is to understand the message being sent to you. The next most important responsibility is to let the person know you got the message. Until this loop is completed, communication has not really occurred; only transmission has. The message must be sent from the sender to the receiver, and confirmation must go back to the sender from the receiver. Then you have two-way communication.

If you are having trouble with communication on one of your projects, try instituting the "say-back rule." It works like this. John, one of your project team members, says something to you. Before you can say what you want to say, you must say back to John what he has said to you so that he is satisfied you got his message. If he is not satisfied, he must send it again, and you must say it back again. This goes on until he is satisfied. Then you make your point, and he must say it back to you until you are satisfied.

If you are having communication problems, this simple rule will bring them to the surface. People are often appalled at how little they have been hearing and at how hard it is to get points across among team members so that everyone is satisfied with the process. But what the say-back rule also does is subtly begin making you and your project team better listeners and better senders of messages. And that is the name of the game in communication. Try it out—it works.

Keys to Improved Communication

To get ideas across:

    1. Hit others where they are

    2. Make certain the listener knows why your message is important

    3. Keep the other person posted

    4.Communicate assertively with understanding

To be a better listener:

    1. Be prepared to listen

    2. Stop talking

    3. Listen with understanding

    4. Hear the speaker out completely

    5. Listen for what is not said

    6. Listen for how something is said

    7. Wait out pauses

    8. Provide feedback

Figure 7.4

CONCLUSION

The things you can do to get your message across and the things you can do to make sure you hear what others are saying are not necessarily complex, dramatic, or difficult. Anyone can do them.

The only trick is that you have to use these ideas for them to work. You can start to use these ideas right away. You don't have to wait for anyone else to do anything differently. Working hard at sending your ideas more effectively and at being a better listener will not only make you a better communicator but will also improve the communication skills of others on your project team. So don't say, ''All right, I'll try.'' Rather, say, ''OK, I'll begin using these ideas today. Here's what I'll do. . . .''

8

Rule Number Eight

BUILD AGREEMENTS THAT VITALIZE TEAM MEMBERS

BUILD AGREEMENTS THAT VITALIZE
TEAM MEMBERS

Disagreements are unavoidable in managing projects. Studies show that project managers spend nearly half their time managing differences. A major reason for this is that project management requires coordinating and integrating the work of many different people, most of whom do not report directly to you. Consequently, you need to manage differences skillfully, but doing so requires working to forge agreements. This approach requires that you see the proverbial clear glass of water filled to the middle as half full and not as half empty.

The existence of disagreement and conflicts in a project is not only unavoidable; it is quite desirable. Conflicts ensure continued interest and commitment, encourage novel and integrative solutions, and focus attention on potential difficulties. Energy is created by conflict.

Conflicts are born out of caring. People do not fight about issues they don't care about. And conflict is a force that potentially unleashes people's imagination. Inherently, conflict is neither good nor bad; rather, the outcomes of conflict can be good or bad, functional or harmful, positive or negative. Marriage and family counselors often find couples divorcing because there is no conflict between the partners. At their worst they take each other for granted. The same thing can happen on your project team. Conflict is a process to be managed, not eliminated.

> Conflicts mean people care!
> Conflict is a process to be
> **managed,** not eliminated.

Figure 8.1

SOURCES OF CONFLICT IN PROJECTS

Many of the sources of conflict derive directly from the inherent nature of projects. Conflicts occur at various points during a project and over a variety of issues. You should take note of both where and when disagreements are likely to arise to manage them most effectively. Project managers report that conflicts typically arise over the following points of contention:

- *Project priorities*. Participants have different views about the proper sequence of activities and tasks. Figure 8.2 shows the cartoon characters Dagwood and Blondie at odds over this type of issue. Such differences occur not only within the project team but also between the project team and other support groups.
- *Administrative procedures*. Disagreements arise over how a project will be managed—for example, over the definition of the project manager's reporting relationships and responsibilities, operational requirements, interdepartmental work agreements, and levels of administrative support.
- *Technical opinions*. The less routine a project, the more likely it is that there are differences of opinions about the ''best way'' to accomplish the project objectives. Disagreements may arise over specifications, technical trade-offs, and techniques to achieve the required performance. For ex-

Blondie □ Young and Raymond

Figure 8.2   (Reprinted with special permission of King Features Syndicate, Inc.)

ample, the director and the film editor on a movie project may have entirely different and competing viewpoints on how best to achieve a certain effect with the camera.

- *Staffing and resource allocations.* Conflicts arise over how best to allocate people to various projects and within project assignments. One project member complains that she always gets the "grunt work" while others get the glamorous assignments. Not only do individuals disagree over which projects their functional manager should assign them to, but they also face competing demands from their project and functional managers. This leads to both interpersonal strife and personal stress.
- *Costs and budgets.* "How much is this going to cost?" and "Why is this costing so much?" are frequent sources of disagreement throughout a project. These differences often arise because it is difficult to estimate costs in the face of uncertainty. A functional support group, for example, may see the funds allocated by the project manager as insufficient for the work requested.
- *Schedules.* A constant source of tension is "How long is this going to take?" The difficulty arises because so often we are dealing with estimates about the future, and the future can seldom be predicted with certainty. At the other extreme, taking into account all the contingencies—all the things that could happen—would prevent the task from getting accomplished. Further, tension is often generated around the sequencing of events, as in the case of "Finish the documentation on this project before starting to program the next portion of the new accounting system."
- *Interpersonal and personality clashes.* Conflicts arise not just over technical issues but also over "style" or "ego-centered" issues like status, power, control, self-esteem, and friendships. Such conflicts may be based on differences that emerge from departmental or organizational factors like varying work goals and time horizons.

MANAGING CONFLICTS OVER THE PROJECT LIFE CYCLE

Our studies, as well as those of other researchers, indicate that the conflict intensity for each of these sources of conflict varies over the life cycle of a project. The tension points can often be predicted and in such cases managed more effectively. These differences are summarized graphically in Figure 8.3.

During the *formative phase*, most conflicts arise over schedules, costs, priorities, and staffing. One reason that these four issues create so much turmoil is that project managers have limited control over other

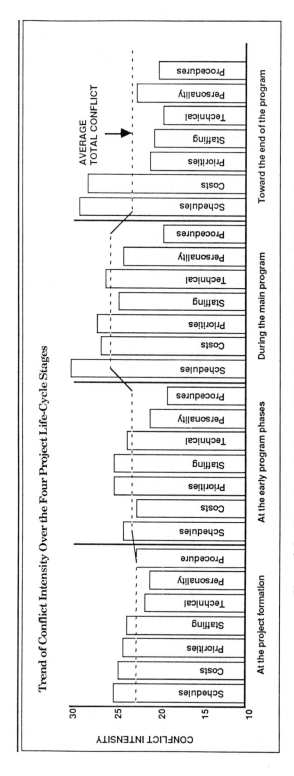

Figure 8.3 (From Barry Z. Posner, "What's All the Fighting About? Conflicts in Project Management," *IEEE Transactions in Engineering Management, 33*, no. 4 (1986), 207–211. © 1986 by IEEE.)

areas that affect these issues, particularly the functional support departments. To minimize detrimental conflict, intensive planning prior to launching the project is essential. Keeping the project goal clearly in mind goes a long way toward minimizing disruptive conflicts. Involving all parties affected by the project can help not only to anticipate potential sources of conflict but also to begin building the team spirit necessary to resolve the differences that will occur. Think about the fact that relay teams in track run the race hundreds of times in practice before they ever step up to the starting blocks.

As a project enters the *early program phase*, conflicts arise primarily over scheduling, priorities, staffing, and technical issues. It is critical to provide feedback on how the project is progressing and to celebrate and reward early accomplishments. Frequent meetings and status review sessions help to develop interpersonal relationships that may be called upon in later, more stressful stages of the project. As the project develops, so should contingency planning about key administrative and procedural issues. It is much easier, for example, to discuss how a problem should be resolved and to work out a procedure for handling differences before rather than after the battle lines have been drawn. Research studies also indicate that the greater the uncertainty about the ''correct'' way to do the job, the more you must employ problem-solving techniques that bring people face to face rather than impersonal processes like rules and regulations.

Every effort should be made to integrate as early as possible (if not right at the start) the various functional groups affected by the project. Every new product development team at companies like Hewlett-Packard and Convergent Technologies contains at least one person from marketing, engineering, and manufacturing. At Mervyn's Department Stores, the weekly advertising supplement is put together by the various department store managers, merchandise buyers, and marketing and financial personnel.

The *main phase* of the project finds most conflicts arising over scheduling issues. Resolving these conflicts requires continual efforts to keep people posted and to monitor work in progress. Technical issues should be resolved early in the process with an emphasis on preliminary technical testing by all involved. Forecasting, thinking ahead, and communicating staffing requirements and changes can make life somewhat less hectic and less anxiety-prone.

As the *end of the project* approaches, conflicts will develop over costs and schedules. It is important to keep team members focused on these issues. If they feel a sense of ownership in the project, they will more naturally identify with the project's success and contribute to it. Focusing on the eventual accomplishment and its significance can also tap in to people's sense of pride. Noah and his new crew must have spent considerable time dreaming about the exciting possibilities before them as they waited for the waters to recede.

Letting people know what life will be like after the project is over helps keep them focused. You may also need to loosen up high-stress environments by not taking yourself or the situation too seriously. Football coach Bill Walsh of the San Francisco 49ers played bellhop for members of his team when they arrived at their hotel before the 1983 Super Bowl game.

BUILDING TO AGREEMENT

When differences arise, you can try to reach an agreement in many ways. These include (1) giving in to the other person, (2) smoothing over the disagreements, (3) suppressing the points of contention, (4) splitting the difference, (5) arguing, (6) persuading, and (7) finding a common ground on which to bargain and negotiate differences. As a project manager, the problem of persuading another person or department to adopt your point of view or to go along with your requests for project support is complicated by the fact that you typically do not possess the "power of the hierarchy." In other words, you lack formal authority. You are not the other person's boss, and you have no right to command or give orders that others are expected or obligated to follow.

One method for gaining acceptance of your viewpoint is to provide a sound rationale for your position. This is the power of intellect or expertise. People generally go along with an individual who is perceived to know what he or she is talking about. The expression of expertise consists of communicating your rationale with reasoning and logic. Within functional areas this tactic may prove useful, but project managers typically operate in more than one functional area. It is difficult to have expertise across many disciplines, but you should try to be conversant across functional areas. Effective project managers are perceived by people in each functional area as knowing something about their discipline and appreciating their point of view.

The more significant problem with trying to rely on reason and logic in managing differences is, quite simply, that rationality does not always prevail. Logic, data, and reason do not always point to a clear solution agreeable to another party. Competing points of view cannot be resolved by logic when each is based on a sound rationale. A likely scenario involves people from different technical backgrounds (for example, computer programming and marketing, or financial analysis and production, or the teenager in junior high school and grandparent at home) who must arrive at a common course of action. But the basis for their discussion is so divergent that satisfactory resolution on common ground is nearly impossible. In such difficult situations, four tactics can help you build agreements in which the parties participate:

1. Create a common ground.
2. Enlarge areas of agreement.
3. Gather information.
4. Focus on issues, not personalities.

1. *Create a common ground.* The most important step in building agreement is to form a strong foundation: What do you and the other person already have in common? What do the two of you agree on? What are you both trying to accomplish? Ideally, the goal of the project should sum up the common ground.

What you want to keep in mind is what you have in common, not what you disagree on. Pushing people apart at the start of a dialogue seldom engenders an atmosphere of cooperation. In agreeing on a common ground, people highlight their necessary interdependencies. When my success is a function of your success and vice versa, we are both more likely to listen and work through our differences than when our successes are independent. This is, of course, one of the reasons why you should work so hard at the start of a project to involve all of the affected parties in determining the project's goal and creating a schedule (and visible schedule document) that underscores the interdependencies.

2. *Enlarge areas of agreement.* The second step is to build on these areas of agreement. This involves moving out of the "selling your idea" or "if I can only convince them!" mode of thinking. The key to the transition from debating to building is an exchange of statements. Instead of point-and-counterpoint debates, you need to make statements and encourage the other person to do the same, such as "If you would be willing to do X, I would be willing to do Y." This can be very hard to do because our egos get deeply entangled in our positions. That is why you need to let go of positions in the first place and find common ground on the project, which can guide the negotiation.

A certain amount of time is needed to allow each person to get his or her ideas out on the table. Too often, however, participants in a conflict continue attacking and defending and devote little time to building an agreement. The building process is facilitated when we (1) allow each person to state his or her position without interruption, (2) allow a brief period of time for questions of clarification only, and (3) ask the question "How can each of us get what we want?" When arguing is leading nowhere, the skilled negotiator switches to statements of possible exchange. Asking "How can each of us get what we want?" transforms the argument into a discussion and the potential deadlock into a settlement.

3. *Gather information.* An important problem-solving technique in managing conflicts during projects is the gathering of information. Working through fundamental issues—such as "Who is in conflict?" "Who can resolve the conflict?" and "Is all the information available?"—helps to create a working foundation for dialogue. If you cannot agree which parties are really involved in the conflict, some important points of view may not be represented in the negotiations. The needs of these people will not in turn be represented in the proposed solutions.

Likewise, too often you will be arguing about, say, a scheduling problem that you and the other person cannot resolve. Disagreements about "what should have happened" often fall into this category. Discussing who should be involved in the negotiation is one way of determining what types of information are needed to build an agreement. This technique forces you to consider "Who will be affected by this agreement?" Research clearly shows that people are most likely to follow through on an agreement that they have helped shape.

4. *Focus on issues, not personalities.* Finally, it is crucial to depersonalize the conflict. When you feel that you have to defend yourself from personal attack, your response typically takes one of two forms. Either you fight back, which only escalates the disagreement and makes the possibility of finding common ground negligible, or you flee. In the latter case, you don't get people to commit their energies to problem solving. Although they may agree to an action, they will have no real commitment to follow through once you are out of sight. What do the mice do when the cat is away? In a fight, the other person's energies are devoted to getting back at you and not to solving the problem.

One of the best ways to focus on issues and not personalities is to be future-oriented: "What are we going to do about this?" rather than "Why can't you be more responsible?" or "Who got us into this situation?" By being future-oriented, you emphasize building agreement on a future course of action rather than blaming each other for past problems. This is not to say that you don't want to explore the past for insight into the causes of problems, but emphasizing the past often leads to one person

```
                        ┌─────────────────────────────┐
                        │  It's US against the problem, │
                        │  not against one another.     │
   Figure 8.4           └─────────────────────────────┘
```

having to defend his or her actions or blame and scapegoat someone else. "What are we going to do to ensure that this doesn't happen again?" is a statement of allies *against the problem*, not against each other.

SUCCESSFUL NEGOTIATORS OF CONFLICT

It is clear that successful project managers are effective negotiators in managing differences. Much has been written about how successful negotiators behave—what they do and what they try to avoid doing as they build agreement between people with differences. Management consultant Clifford Bolster reports in his studies that technically trained managers frequently discover that they rely too heavily on reasoning and logic in trying to get others to do what they want. He observes, "Negotiation is a process that may be used when logical reasoning has run its course, and represents a critical skill for the technical manager today."

The objective of negotiation is to reach an agreement that satisfies both parties. Satisfaction is an *emotional*, not a logical, experience. Negotiation is not an optimal, dispassionate problem-solving experience where analysis and reasoning are the only skills needed to determine the cause of the problem and to reach the solution with the highest probability of solving the problem. Imagine whether Noah could have *proved* that it would rain for 40 days and 40 nights or whether this really would have flooded the earth.

The best solution in negotiations is the one that satisfies both parties and results in committed follow-through on the solution. This is not to suggest that analytical skills are not needed in negotiation, just that they are not paramount. They take up time and get in the way of efforts that could be devoted to building an agreement.

Since good project managers must be skillful negotiators, each of the following nine techniques should be part of your repertoire.

1. *Be direct.* Act rather than react. Be a problem finder. Be clear about your interests and needs.

2. *Label behavior.* For clarity, make prefacing remarks during the negotiation. "What I'd like to do is propose . . ." and "May I make the suggestion that . . ." reduces ambiguity about your intentions.

3. *Avoid argument.* Argument during the negotiation dilutes the process and gets people off the track of searching for and building upon agreements. Remember, arguments are emotional. They are seldom resolved with logic and facts.

4. *Be aware of the limitations of logic.* Rather than rely too heavily on logic and reason, try this attitude: "What seems reasonable to you is reasonable to me." Exchange statements play a pivotal role in this process. Sensitivity to others' perceptions is vital.

5. *Know what you want and ask for it.* If you don't know what you want, you can't ask for it. If you don't ask for it, you're not likely to get it. Nobody can read your mind, nor can you read anyone else's mind. Assertive expressions of needs, interests, and possible exchanges move the negotiations along.

6. *Repeat expectations firmly.* Persist in stating expectations, wants, and needs and in not letting the other person off too easily or making it easy for them to say no. By building on common ground, make it possible for the other person to say yes.

7. *Don't justify.* Too often, justification seems like rationalization and clutching at straws. Rather than justify defensively, make firm assertions backed by facts when appropriate.

8. *Avoid "irritants."* Words and phrases like "Anyone could see that," "It's always been done this way," "my generous offer," and the like push the other party into a corner where their only option is to fight or flee. Keep the discussion focused on the issues and not on personalities.

9. *Create alternative solutions.* Understand that both your own interests and those of the other person can probably be satisfied by more than one solution. Imagination is required both to understand and to use what you have that the other person wants or needs, and vice versa. Often this entails numerous "What if?" statements. Inflate trial balloons and float them for possible agreement.

CONCLUSION

By effectively managing and negotiating conflicts, you will achieve positive outcomes from the inevitable differences that arise in project management. You can get the job done most effectively when you build agreements that vitalize participants. Conflict creates energy that is vital to managing projects from inception to implementation. Anticipating the sources of conflict and understanding the ebb and flow of conflicts in a project environment will increase your ability to harness this energy. Paradoxically, finding—or, if necessary, creating—areas of agreement is an important starting place for negotiating differences.

Figure 8.5

> The objective of negotiations is to reach an agreement that satisfies both parties, and is a win for the project. Satisfaction is an emotional, not a logical, experience.

9

Rule Number Nine

EMPOWER YOURSELF AND OTHERS ON THE PROJECT TEAM

Rule Number Nine

EMPOWER YOURSELF AND OTHERS ON THE PROJECT TEAM

Everybody wants power. Few people feel they have enough of it—especially project managers! Haven't you heard these laments? "If I only had the authority necessary to get those people on track . . ." "If only I had the power to influence my superiors . . ." "What I need to get this done is more authority." No matter what level of managers we have worked with, regardless of setting or function, all have felt that their situation would be better if only they had *more power*.

We have all been taught to associate power with authority and with one's location in the hierarchy of an organization—in other words, "position power." This is a restricted view of power. It assumes that power is a fixed-sum commodity and that there is only so much to go around. This viewpoint is limiting and contrary to what powerful project managers understand: that power is dynamic, and like electricity it is all around us, virtually infinite in its potential. Our challenge is to find ways to tap in to this energy and to harness and channel its forces. Like putting money in the bank, power is a source of credit that expands with use and makes other people feel stronger and richer, too.

Literally, the word *power* means "to be able." Making something happen arises at least as much from personal competencies as it does from resources associated with one's position. Professor Michael Badawy argues in his book *Developing Managerial Skills in Engineers and Scientists* that "of the two types of power, positional and personal, the project manager's authority is actually based on power which largely

Effective project managers
know how to use personal
power to get the job done.

Figure 9.1

stems more from his personal abilities and less from his position.'' The power that project managers use is based on an understanding of the reciprocal relationship between leaders and their followers.

Personal power is a set of skills and abilities possessed by an individual. It refers to ways we work with and respond to others in face-to-face situations. Most important, it does not come with an ''office'' but travels with each individual.

WHERE POWER COMES FROM

Traditionally, power has been conceptualized as coming from one of five sources:

1. *Reward* power, based on our perception that another person has the ability to reward or grant resources that we desire.
2. *Coercive* power, based on our perception that another person has the ability to punish or withhold valued resources from us.
3. *Legitimate* power, based on our internalized belief that another person, like the ''boss,'' has the legitimate right to request certain types of actions and that we have a social obligation to comply with the request; often called ''institutional power'' or ''formal authority.''
4. *Referent* power, based on our desire to identify with another person and our belief that going along with the person's requests will facilitate a favorable interpersonal relationship and foster mutual respect.
5. *Expert* power, based on our perception that the other person has some special knowledge or information relevant to the task or problem at hand.

The first three sources of power (reward, coercive, and legitimate) form the basis of position power. They are lodged in the position that the person holds. The last two (referent and expert) form the sources of personal power. They reside in the personal characteristics of the position holder. There are limits to the amount of position power that you can use. For example, how many times can you fire someone? How often can you give someone a raise or promotion? And, more important, how often does a project manager even have this kind of power? By contrast, there is virtually no limit to the amount of personal power that one person may possess in relation to another.

HOW POWER IS DISTRIBUTED

Researchers who have investigated why one branch, department, or unit of a company is more effective than another similar branch, department, or unit working under identical company policies, procedures, and organizational structures have identified power and its distribution as a key factor.

A consistent finding is that managers in the underachieving units hoard power. In the high-performing units, the managers share power. Consequently, people at every level in the high-performing units feel that they can, and should, be responsible for their unit's effectiveness. Contemporary management thought holds that it is powerlessness that corrupts and not vice versa. Consider what the advertisement for the New United Motors Manufacturing, Inc., plant in Fremont, California (a joint venture between General Motors and Toyota) in Figure 9.2 suggests: When people feel that they have power, they feel that they can make a difference, and productivity improves. Noah's teammates probably felt that if they didn't think something was right, they could take this up directly to the top!

Another study of project managers reported several significant relationships between project performance and the use of various power bases. For example, the less project personnel perceived project managers as using position power and the more they perceived managers as using personal power, the greater were the levels of project involvement and openness of upward communication and the higher was the productivity of the project team. Similar findings emerge from other studies involving such diverse occupations as sales personnel, college teachers, insurance underwriters, postal service carriers, and assembly-line workers.

GUIDELINES FOR THE EFFECTIVE USE OF POWER

People respond in one of three ways when you use power. They may demonstrate *commitment* to your request and enthusiastically engage in the requisite behavior. They may *comply*; they go along with your request because they feel they have to, but they probably do not do anything beyond what is minimally required. Or they may *resist* by failing to

Figure 9.2   (Reprinted with permission of Chevrolet Motor Division.)

follow through or by fighting back. Obviously, you need to understand how the various power bases can be used to generate commitment or, at least, willing compliance rather than resistance to your requests.

Building and Using Referent Power

You develop referent power when others on the project respect and admire you personally. This source of power is determined by the way you treat people. For example, showing consideration for their needs and feelings, dealing with each person fairly, and standing up for the group are ways to increase referent power. Face-to-face interaction with each individual on the team is essential.

Another way you create referent power is by setting an example. You should intentionally set an example of what you expect and want from others. For example, if quality is important, you need to emphasize quality in all you do, from the products you produce to the correspondence you send out. If quality is important, make it the first item on every meeting's agenda and the first question you ask when reviewing the project's progress with individuals on the team. Whenever Noah met with God, what do you think they talked about first? A major reason for Noah's commitment to the ark project was his trust (faith) in God.

Building and Using Expert Power

You can't influence other people just because you're the technical expert. Others must recognize that you have expertise and perceive you to be a credible source of information and advice. Several factors help facilitate this process—for example, making sure that others are aware of your formal education, relevant work experience, and significant accomplishments. Also, you need to stay current and up-to-date. You cannot maintain an image of expertise unless you keep up with the latest developments in your field and remain professionally active.

Expert power can be undermined by relying too heavily on logic and rational reasoning as persuasion tactics. A barrage of one-way communication often leaves others feeling backed into a corner. Two-way communication, in which you first uncover the feelings and concerns of each person and then deal with these in making a persuasive argument, is more effective. If, for example, people on your project are concerned about the possible unfavorable consequences of a policy, you should propose ways to avoid such consequences or to deal with them if they cannot be avoided.

Also, people react negatively when project managers flaunt their greater expertise and experience. It is usually counterproductive to try to convince others by belittling their arguments or making them feel stupid. This feeling of incompetence can be created when project managers treat the objections, concerns, or suggestions of others as unimportant, trivial, or insignificant. Recognizing the contributions of others, respecting their self-worth, and incorporating, when possible, their ideas into action plans encourages their perception of your expertise (and your good sense).

> Good project managers
> earn the respect of the team
> and tactfully use their
> expert power.

Figure 9.3

Using Legitimate Power

Authority is exercised by making a legitimate request. You will encounter less resistance if you make it easy for others to go along with your request. One way to do this is to make "polite" requests. This is especially important for project personnel who are likely to be sensitive to status differences and authority relationships (for example, someone older than you or someone with multiple supervisors). Polite requests generally include the word *please*.

Another way to make it easy to go along is to explain the reasons behind a request. The Garfield cartoon in Figure 9.4 illustrates this point. Others are more likely to go along with your requests when they see them as consistent with agreed-on task objectives. Sometimes it is helpful to review the decision process you used to arrive at an action plan with the project team. By taking them through the process step by step, they can see why the decision was made and why other alternatives were rejected.

Finally, it is helpful when project personnel understand that your requests are within the scope of your authority. Linking requests with official documentation such as written rules, policies, contract provisions, and schedules is one way to do this. Just like Noah, it may not be sufficient to say, "Trust me." It helps when subordinates perceive that a higher authority is on your side.

Figure 9.4   (© 1983 United Feature Syndicate, Inc.)

Using Reward Power

The most common way of using reward power is to offer tangible rewards to people if they go along with your requests. However, the ideal conditions for using reward power effectively seldom exist. Many project managers lack control over attractive tangible rewards. Project participants often have interdependent tasks that make it difficult to use individual incentives. Furthermore, objective indicators of performance are not available for many kinds of tasks, and people's behavior is often not easily observable.

There are other problems with relying too heavily on rewards as a source of influence. You may obtain compliance with rules and policies by the promise of rewards, but you are unlikely to win the person's heart or commitment. Professor Gary Yukl in his book *Leadership in Organizations* points out these problems. As he notes, when people perform tasks in order to obtain a promised reward, they perceive their behavior as a means to an end. This may tempt them to take shortcuts and neglect less visible aspects of the task in order to complete the assignment and obtain the reward. Few internal incentives are generated to motivate the individual to put forth any effort beyond what is required or to demonstrate any particular initiative in carrying out the task. Subsequently, their relationship with the project manager tends to be defined in purely economic terms. Special rewards come to be expected every time something new or unusual is required. Most managers run out of tangible goodies, especially as expectations escalate. In addition, using reward power can lead to resistance and resentment because people feel they are being manipulated by the contingent ("I will do this if you do that") nature of the relationship.

Consequently, rather than using rewards as explicit incentives, effective project managers use them more subtly to recognize and reinforce desired behavior. They focus on rewarding intrinsic needs like recognition, self-esteem, and future opportunities for growth and challenge.

The use of reward power should supplement and strengthen your referent power base. Give rewards in a way that expresses your personal appreciation for project members' efforts and accomplishments. Studies show that recipients of rewards come to like people who repeatedly provide rewards in an acceptable manner. Interpersonal relationships are more satisfying when they are viewed as an expression of mutual friendship and loyalty rather than an impersonal economic exchange.

Using Coercive Power

Effective project managers try to avoid using coercive power except when absolutely necessary because it is likely to create resentment and erode their personal power base. With coercion there is no chance of gaining commitment. Even willing compliance is difficult to achieve.

Coercion is most appropriate when it is used to stop behavior detrimental to the organization (e.g., theft, sabotage, violation of safety rules, or insubordination). Strategies of "positive discipline," rather than scaring people with threats or sample doses of punishment, are directed toward inducing subordinates to assume responsibility for helping to resolve the discipline problem. Here are some guidelines for using positive discipline:

- Let people know about the rules and penalties for violations.
- Administer discipline consistently and promptly.
- Provide sufficient warning before resorting to punishment.
- Get the facts before using reprimands or punishments.

- Stay calm and avoid appearing hostile.
- Use appropriate punishments.
- Administer warnings and punishments in private.

Figure 9.5

> With Position Power:
>
> - Stay within your authority
> - Rewards are more than money; try praise
> - Coercive power should be used sparingly

WHAT PEOPLE WANT FROM THEIR LEADERS

It is apparent that among the sources of power, the central determinant is in the "eye of the beholder"—what counts is what others (your subordinates, peers, and associates) perceive. The way you handle yourself, project members' interactions with you, your managerial style, and the like influence their perception of your power and hence the effect you can have on their behavior.

What do others expect of you? What do people expect from their leaders? A series of studies involving thousands of managers have identified four personal characteristics that people admire, look for, and expect most from those whom they are *willing* to follow. What do you think these characteristics are? Think about how you would measure up in the eyes of your project team.

The most frequently mentioned characteristic is *honesty*. People want a leader who is truthful with them and can be trusted. People judge your honesty by observing your behavior. Do you do what you say you are going to do, or not?

Sam Walton, founder and chairman of Wal-Mart Stores—rated by *Forbes* as the richest man in the country—told his employees that if they achieved their profit objectives, he would put on a hula skirt and dance down Wall Street. They did. And he did! Being honest is, of course, a game involving risk. The leader must be the first one to ante up.

The Eye of the Follower:

The personal traits people want most
from their superiors are

    Honesty

    Competence

    Direction

    Inspiration

Figure 9.6

The second most desired characteristic in leaders is *competence.* Before they will follow a request, people must believe that this person knows what he or she is doing. This does not necessarily involve functional or technical abilities. The specific kind of competence followers look for is affected by many factors, including position in the hierarchy and economic condition of the company. As a project manager, you must also be willing to demonstrate your ability to recognize the competence or expertise of others around you. In doing so, you demonstrate your level of trust in others—not unlike the kind of trust you want others to feel toward you.

The third most frequently mentioned characteristic is *a sense of direction.* This trait should be a natural for project managers. Leaders are expected to be forward-looking, to know where they are going, and to be concerned about the future of the enterprise. Followers want to have a feeling for the destination that the leader has in mind: Where are we going? What will it be like there? For example, when your project takes you to a foreign location, what do you do? Get a map. Read about the place. Look at pictures. Talk to others who have been there. Seek professional advice about the important sites, customs, or regulations. Find out where (or what) to eat, where to stay, where to shop. The project manager's clarity about the target and the project objectives are akin to the magnetic north of a compass. They pull the project team forward and keep it on course.

Finally, people expect leaders to be *inspiring.* It is important that the project manager be seen as enthusiastic, energetic, and positive about the project. Apple Computer manager Dave Patterson put it this way: "The leader is the evangelist for the dream."

Nora Watson, an editor, offers this viewpoint in Studs Turkel's book *Working*: "I think most people are looking for a calling, not a job. Most of us have jobs that are too small for our spirit." Her statement is a reminder that you must help the people on your project team find a greater sense of purpose and worth in their day-to-day life on the job. Effective project managers inspire confidence in their project personnel about the correctness of "going along." They do this by their personal conviction and commitment to the project and by their actions.

To empower your project team, help them find a greater sense of purpose and worth in their day-to-day life on the project.

Figure 9.7

CONCLUSION

What does it mean to be honest? To be competent? To be forward-looking and inspirational? These characteristics are the essence of *credibility*. When you are perceived as trustworthy, as knowing what you are talking about, as dynamic and sincere, and as having a sense of direction, others will see you as credible. And when you have credibility, people are likely to comply with your requests and even more likely to demonstrate a sense of commitment in their follow-through regardless of the power source you tap in to. Both you and others will feel empowered! This is how you turn your GO-CART into a super-charged, fuel-injected machine and get the job done.

10

Rule Number Ten

ENCOURAGE RISK
TAKING AND CREATIVITY

Rule Number Ten

ENCOURAGE RISK TAKING AND CREATIVITY

To remain competitive in the marketplace, every organization must be innovative. It is essential that every organization encourage risk taking and creativity. Project teams are often set up for the sole purpose of spurring process and product breakthroughs.

Creativity can be influenced. Many of the factors that have been identified as facilitating or hindering creative behavior can be affected by the organization and by the project manager. Innovative behavior in organizations is not simply a matter of selection, training, or good fortune. John Couch, who headed the original Lisa design team for Apple Computer, offers these ''banners of innovation'' for project teams:

- It's more fun to be a pirate than to join the Navy.
- Don't argue about diamonds and emeralds when the rest of the world has coal.
- The reward is in the journey.
- When two people agree on the same thing, one of them is unnecessary.
- Build products that we ourselves want.

We can look at the issue of creativity and innovation from the perspective of both the organization and the individual project member. But first it is useful to explore what factors block creativity and how these might be handled.

BLOCKS TO CREATIVITY

Creative behavior is the expression of creative ability. One reason for the absence of creative behavior may be that people on your project team feel inhibited from expressing their talents. Anxiety, fear of evaluation, defensiveness, and cultural inhibition are all blocks to the realization of creative potential. Managerial practices and organizational policies that foster such negative reactions hinder the expression of creative talent.

Organizations that stress the consequences of failure rather than the rewards for success tend to inhibit the expression of new ideas. Conversely, a climate that supports risk taking adopts the attitude of Thomas Edison: "I failed my way to success." Paul Cook, chief executive officer at the highly innovative Raychem Corporation, puts it this way: "What gives me the greatest delight is the constant outpouring of new ideas." Or as Bob Metcalfe, founder of 3COM, explains: "We tell our people to make ten mistakes a day. If they're not, then they're not trying hard enough!"

Organizational instability can also inhibit creative expression. Unstable organizations are unpredictable to their members and breed insecurity and anxiety. But don't try to achieve stability through excessive formalization of rules, policies, relationships, and procedures. High levels of formalization interfere with interunit communication and discourage experimentation or the seeking of new alternatives or methods. Centralization restricts the free exchange of information and slows communication. These delays tend to dampen enthusiasm, increase response times, and heighten the probability that information is lost or distorted. A highly centralized organization structure may inhibit the early stages of creativity and innovation.

Finally, leave time in the project for thinking and experimenting, for creative behavior. Take the attitude "Don't just do something, sit there." The creative process takes time; how much time is not clear. When a manager views creativity as an unprogrammed activity, the proposition "programmed work drives out unprogrammed work" comes into play. In such circumstances, the probability that project participants have little time for creative efforts is high. The highly innovative 3M Company guards against this by institutionalizing the bootlegging process. It expects all engineers and scientists to spend 15 percent of their time working on nonprogrammed activities. The IDEA program at Texas Instruments provides "on-the-spot" seed money to finance long-shot projects. The project does not need to obtain top management's approval.

> The creative process
> takes time;
> so build the time
> into your projects.

Figure 10.1

FACILITATING CREATIVITY AND INNOVATION

Studies have identified reinforcement, goals, deadlines (like milestones), extended efforts, and freedom as facilitating creative efforts. By developing policies and practices that encourage individual creativity, you can develop and maintain higher levels of innovation.

Creative behavior, like any other type of behavior, is influenced by its outcome. When you ignore or punish risk taking, or when creative efforts are stifled, threatened, ridiculed, or stolen, creative energies are likely to be diminished. Even if creative talent has lain dormant, you can resurrect it through training and reinforcement. Often, you just have to let it out of the bottle. People have sometimes viewed creativity, like virtue, as its own reward. Certainly the intrinsic rewards in the satisfaction and feelings of accomplishment that accompany a creative insight or endeavor are powerful. Yet creative individuals, from scientists to toddlers, respond to extrinsic reinforcement as well.

Creative individuals need and respond to recognition, praise, and rewards. Few novels and even fewer (if any) scientific articles are published anonymously; composers copyright their music; artists sign their works. Inside the cover of Apple's Macintosh computer are the signatures of its entire design team.

Much of the world's great art, sculpture, and music has been produced on commission, as have many of the world's commercial innovations. Commissions not only provide monetary incentives, but they also facilitate innovation by setting guidelines as to expectations and deadlines for what is to be produced and when it is to be completed. Massive efforts in technological innovation grew from President Kennedy's goal of putting a man on the moon by 1970. Mozart finished one of the world's greatest operas by working through the night preceding its premiere. In many fields, time pressures can be outrageous *and* productive. It has been said that creative people in advertising work best

> Clear goals and deadlines
> help foster creativity.
> But encouraging an
> atmosphere of risk taking
> is just as important.

Figure 10.2

while "under the gun." Deadlines and creativity are not necessarily in conflict.

Of course, the imposition of tight deadlines can be carried too far and can force acceptance of the first creative response. Evidence abounds that conscious efforts to avoid the immediate acceptance of obvious solutions can enhance creative effort. In one study, for example, groups worked on problems until they arrived at a solution. They were then instructed to put that solution aside and to derive a second one. Invariably, the second solutions were superior to the first, more conventional ones.

Individuals must be free to create. However, freedom and autonomy can be interpreted in vastly different ways. Certainly freedom from ridicule and fear is important, as are the opportunity and the time to engage in preparation, incubation, reflection, and other elements of the creative process. Yet freedom and autonomy do not necessarily mean abandoning guidelines or constraints. Contrary to popular belief, creative individuals can live within budgets. One report analyzed 567 technical innovations in products or processes that occurred in 121 companies in five manufacturing industries. More than two-thirds cost less than $100,000; only 2 percent cost over $1 million. Individuals with complete freedom seldom get on track; among technical personnel, goals, budgets, and guidelines generally facilitate rather than hinder the creative process. The freedom in this case focuses on how to pursue an assignment as it relates to organizational goals.

Like any desired behavior, creativity must be identified, actively encouraged, recognized, rewarded, and used. Your challenge is to exercise sensitivity as to how best to provide reinforcement, goals and deadlines, extended effort, and a measure of freedom and autonomy in order to encourage creativity. Would the ark have ever been built on time or all the animals assembled two by two if Noah had wanted to approve every decision that was made? Clarity about the goal releases people's energies to pursue their tasks with enthusiasm.

Figure 10.3

> Deadlines and creativity
> are not necessarily in conflict.

Projects that have clear, operational objectives tend to provide goals and deadlines that aid creativity and innovation. The maxim "Necessity is the mother of invention" rings true. Project personnel who do not know what is necessary seldom find creative and innovative solutions to problems. One study noted that project managers in successful high-technology firms encouraged their product development engineers to get out into the field. Unless this happens, there is a danger that the marketing identification of an opportunity will not get translated down to the product development engineers in a way that they can appreciate.

Similarly, when you support your project team and tolerate risk taking (and even failure), you can develop a climate in which high levels of creativity and innovation abound. Studies of managers who achieved extraordinary results in their organizations point out that people must be willing to risk making a mistake: "Those who want everything to be right the first time will never take the risk of innovating."

Creative behavior deals in uncertainty, which requires support and frequent communication at the interpersonal level. Fostering an open exchange of information and promoting exposure to new ideas enhance creative efforts. The Eleventh Commandment at the 3M Company is "Thou shalt not kill a new product idea." A great example of this is their Post-It notes, which everyone seems to find indispensable today. Initial reaction to the product was, "It's silly." Market surveys were negative. But the people at 3M continued to work with the idea for years until it began to gain acceptance—and a $300 million product was born.

There is evidence as well that both flexibility and complexity in organizational design enhance the creative process. Flexibility permits the organization to adopt new and different ways of doing things. Complexity promotes specialization and autonomy. This means that project teams should be made up of individuals with diverse backgrounds and different specialties. This diversity stimulates creative productivity. Diversity provides people with opportunities to come up with new combinations and associations of ideas, provided they are encouraged or at least permitted to interact across the boundaries of their fields of expertise.

DEVELOPING BETTER IDEAS

Everyone has the potential to be creative. Keep this in mind when projects get bogged down and out of synch or when a timely innovative solution is required to a difficult problem. You can either inhibit or facilitate creative expression.

You should be on guard for the myriad "killer phrases" that crop up and tend to dampen creative energies. When pushed to their logical extremes, all of the examples in Figure 10.4 are illogical. Like any new seedling, a new idea needs space, nourishment, and care until it can stand on its own. Killer phrases stomp on these ideas prematurely. So to the statement "But it's not in the budget!" you might respond "Of course not; we didn't have this idea when the budget was initially proposed" or "Do you mean to say that this organization won't support new ideas?" To the naysayers who exclaim, "We tried that before!" explain to them that "now is different, in the following ways: . . ."

" KILLER PHRASES "

- We tried that before.
- Our place is different.
- It costs too much.
- We don't have the time.
- Let's make a market research test of it first.
- The union will scream.
- It's against company policy.
- Why change it? It's still working o.k.
- You're right but . . .
- Let's form a committee.

Figure 10.4

Four strategies will help you develop better ideas for yourself and your project team:

1. Problem sensitivity
2. Idea fluency
3. Originality
4. Flexibility

1. *Problem sensitivity* is the ability to recognize that a problem exists—to cut through misunderstanding, lack of facts, misconceptions, and other obscuring obstacles and perceive the real problem. One aspect of this is the ability to be a problem finder, not just a problem solver. This requires that you develop early-warning signs or identify potential red flags in the project life cycle that will warn you against the possibility of veering off course or going over a cliff.

One reason we are often problem-insensitive is that we place restraints on problems that don't exist. The famous nine-dot puzzle in Figure 10.5 demonstrates this point. The problem requires you to draw four straight lines through all nine dots without retracing and without lifting your pencil from the paper. This can also be done with only three lines, two lines, and even with one line! Try this puzzle for a moment or two.

Draw four straight lines that
will cross through all nine dots
(without lifting your pencil)

Figure 10.5

What keeps us from solving this problem immediately is a non-existent constraint or boundary—at least from the problem's viewpoint —that we place on the problem. Developing better ideas often requires you to test your assumptions, to go beyond your experiences, and possibly to bend the rules (remember John Couch's remark: "It's more fun to be a pirate than to join the Navy!'').

2. *Idea fluency* is the ability to generate a large number of alternative solutions to a given problem in a given time. It is the law of large numbers, from statistical theory, applied to problem solving. In other words, the more ideas you have, the higher the probability that you will have good ideas. Robert Swerington, former chief executive officer at AMACO, was asked, "Why is your company so much more successful than your competitors at drilling wells which strike oil?" His reply: "Because we drill more wells!''

In a classical brainstorming sense, this is separating idea generation from idea evaluation. Premature evaluation stops the generation of new ideas. Furthermore, scholars of the innovation process have demonstrated quite persuasively that few ideas (concepts, processes, products) are immediate commercial successes. Night lighting for outdoor sports stadiums was several steps removed from the creation of iridescent lighting for ships at sea, and permeable face masks for coal miners were not the original intent of the inventors of disposable brassieres. Noah obviously asked for as many ideas as possible on determining the gender of porcupines besides just trying to pick them up.

3. *Originality* assumes many perspectives. In practical, day-to-day problem solving, complete newness or pure originality is usually not what you need. The originality you require is more likely to be that of finding new ways to vary existing conditions, new ways to adapt existing ideas to new conditions, or a new modification of something to fit an existing condition. Conditions that impede originality include stereotyping, saturation, and failing to use all of our sensory inputs.

Stereotyping is to some extent the difficulty people have in the nine-dot problem. We see a square even when one is not intended. Our imaginations are limited by our tendency to see what we expect to see. As you probably determined, the solution to the nine-dot problem is to go outside the self-imposed boundaries, as shown in Figure 10.6.

Another factor that limits our ability to be original is called "saturation." The more familiar we are with a situation (person, problem), the harder it is for us to see it in another context. Our tendency is to see all problems alike or to see all problems through a single filter (for instance, engineering, accounting, or public relations). For example, look

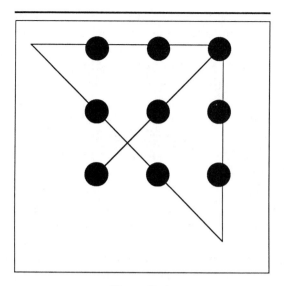

Figure 10.6

at the list of numbers in Figure 10.7. See if you can determine the logic behind their particular sequence.

Difficult? The vast majority of people approach this problem as a "numbers" or mathematical problem because that's the form they found it in. There is no easy numbers solution (if one is even possible!). But if you write out these numbers (for example, 11 becomes *eleven*), the solution becomes immediately apparent. Try it.

Too often we approach problems from a particular point of view, or stereotype, that limits our creative problem-solving ability. It also boxes people and departments in and limits their potential contributions —as in "Engineers can't talk with real customers," "Sales people are more concerned about their customers than they are about this company," or "The accounting department always says no."

You also enrich your problem-solving ability when you use inputs from all your senses (which are interconnected fairly directly). Visuali-

18, 11, 15, 14, 30, 12, 20

What is the logic behind this particular sequencing of numbers?

Figure 10.7

zation seems especially important. Friedrich Kekule, the famous chemist who discovered the structure of the benzene ring, did so in a dream after having devoted considerable conscious thought to its enigmatic structure. A delightful children's book is titled *Put Your Mother on the Ceiling*. Children visualize this quite easily and naturally, but it is this same skill that enables the architect to imagine what a building will look like when completed (and how people will feel as they stroll through its lobby) or a computer programmer to write user-friendly software or the personnel specialist to design stimulating recruitment strategies or Noah to prepare an ark for the Great Flood.

4. *Flexibility* is the willingness to consider a wide variety of approaches to a problem (for example, the interests of all parties involved). Rather than zeroing in on one particular idea, technique, or viewpoint, the flexible project manager starts out by remembering that if one solution won't work, the problem can always be approached from another angle. Occasionally this requires a healthy skepticism about the obvious. As noted earlier, a group's first solution to a problem is generally not as optimal as its second solution. You may have to push the project team to generate that second solution or challenge them to go beyond the initial solution.

Flexibility is akin to idea fluency in asking us to view and understand a problem in different ways. What is the customer's viewpoint? How would this problem be perceived in the budget office? On the manufacturing floor? In the corporate boardroom? In the trade magazines?

Consider the case of the project engineer who was called to the building superintendent's office. The superintendent said that many complaints had been received about the elevators being too slow, and he wanted the engineer to solve this problem. What would you do?

A week passed, and the engineer announced that he had a solution. The superintendent was delighted and expected to hear suggestions about increasing elevator speed, hydraulics, a new algorithm for sequencing the elevators during peak hours, or something similar. Instead the engineer proposed the installation of mirrors on each floor next to the elevators. If people were kept busy checking their appearance, he explained, they would have less time to notice the wait!

The boss had seen the problem as one of speeding up the elevators, but the engineer looked at the problem with flexibility. He chose to attack the impatience of the people waiting rather than the speed of the elevators. By failing to look at problems from different (multiple) perspectives, we often limit our creative potential.

CONCLUSION

Without encouraging risk taking and creativity, it is difficult to imagine how Noah would ever have succeeded in building, launching, and navigating the ark. Getting the job done, except in the most routine situations, always requires some amount of ingenuity. The most stimulating and rewarding projects are somewhat like riding a roller coaster, never really knowing for sure where the dips, twists, and turns are but enjoying the challenge and being confident in our ability to stay on the ride to the end. Like the turtle, the most successful project managers realize that they make significant progress only when they stick their neck out.

Driving to the Checkered Flag

GETTING THE JOB DONE

GETTING THE JOB DONE

So there you have it—ten rules for managing projects to successful completion. Adhering to the first four rules will enable you to develop a sound plan, a plan that is strong yet flexible enough to handle the inevitable unexpected problems. It will be a plan that your project team members can commit themselves to. Your GO-CARTS will be capable of carrying you the distance, to the checkered flag.

The last six rules are designed to help you manage the project plan from beginning to end. They will help you anticipate problems before they become severe enough to knock you out of the race. Unexpected pit stops will be minimized and handled more efficiently because you will be navigating the course as a DRIVER who is well prepared and highly motivated to get to the finish line without crashing.

So the key to going fast later is to go slow early. Take the time to build solid GO-CARTS. For every one of your projects, remember to determine each factor:

Goals for the project
Objectives for the project
Checkpoints to monitor progress
Activities to be completed
Relationships among the activities
Time estimates for the activities
Schedule for the project

Develop your abilities as a DRIVER so that project implementation goes smoothly. This is facilitated when you perform all of the following actions:

<u>D</u>irect people, both individually and as a team
<u>R</u>einforce project team members' excitement and commitment
<u>I</u>nform all people connected with the project
<u>V</u>italize participants by building agreements
<u>E</u>mpower yourself and others
<u>R</u>isk approaching problems creatively

These are the ten rules that successful project managers follow. Now that you know and understand how to apply these rules, the only thing left for you to do is to begin using them.

REFERENCES

REFERENCES

RULE NUMBER ONE

KENNETH BLANCHARD AND SPENCER JOHNSON, *The One Minute Manager* (New York: Morrow, 1982).

JOAN KNUTSON, *How to Be a Successful Project Manager* (New York: American Management Association Extension Institute, 1980).

THOMAS J. PETERS AND ROBERT H. WATERMAN, JR., *In Search of Excellence* (New York: Harper & Row, 1982).

RULE NUMBER TWO

STEVEN KERR, "On the Folly of Rewarding A, While Hoping for B," *Academy of Management Journal*, *18* (1975), 769–783.

ROBERT KREITNER, *Management* (Boston: Houghton-Mifflin, 1983).

RULE NUMBER THREE

KENNETH BLANCHARD AND ROBERT LORBER, *Putting the One Minute Manager to Work* (New York: Morrow, 1984).

LYNN STUCKENBRUCK, *The Implementation of Project Management: The Professional's Handbook* (Reading, Mass.: Addison-Wesley, 1981).

RULE NUMBER FOUR

RALPH L. KLEIN, *The Secrets of Successful Project Management* (New York: Wiley, 1986).

JEROME D. WEIST AND FERDINAND K. LEVY, *A Management Guide to PERT/CPM* (Englewood Cliffs, N.J.: Prentice-Hall, 1977).

MAURICE ZELDMAN, *Keeping Technical Projects on Target* (New York: AMACOM, 1978).

RULE NUMBER FIVE

ROSABETH MOSS KANTER, *The Change Masters* (New York: Simon & Schuster, 1983).

GEORGE E. MANNERS, JR., JOSEPH A. STEGER, AND THOMAS W. ZIMMERER, "Motivating Your R & D Staff," *Research Management*, 26, no. 5 (1983), 12–16.

BARRY Z. POSNER, "Managing High Technology Professionals," in *Handbook of Technology Management*, ed. Dundar E. Kocaogln (New York: Wiley, 1988).

RULE NUMBER SIX

TRACY KIDDER, *The Soul of a New Machine* (Boston: Little, Brown, 1982).

JAMES M. KOUZES AND BARRY Z. POSNER, *The Leadership Challenge: How to Get Extraordinary Things Done in Organizations* (San Francisco: Jossey-Bass, 1987).

GARY N. POWELL AND BARRY Z. POSNER, "Excitement and Commitment: Keys to Project Success," *Project Management Journal*, 15, no. 4 (1984), 39–46.

RULE NUMBER SEVEN

ROBERT E. ALBERTI AND MICHAEL L. EMMONS, *Stand Up, Speak Out, Talk Back!* (New York: Pocket Books, 1975).

CARL R. ROGERS AND RICHARD E. FARSON, "Active Listening," in *Organizational Psychology: Readings on Human Behavior in Organizations*, ed. D. A. Kolb, I. M. Rubin, and J. M. McIntyre (Englewood Cliffs, N.J.: Prentice-Hall, 1984).

RULE NUMBER EIGHT

CLIFFORD F. BOLSTER, "Negotiating: A Critical Skill for Technical Managers," *Research Management*, 27, no. 6 (1984), 18–20.

ROGER FISHER AND WILLIAM URY, *Getting to Yes* (New York: Penguin Books, 1981).

Barry Z. Posner, "What's All the Fighting About? Conflicts in Project Management," *IEEE Transactions in Engineering Management*, *33*, no. 4 (1986), 207–211.

Hans J. Thamhain and David L. Wilemon, "Leadership, Conflict, and Program Management Effectiveness," *Sloan Management Review*, *19*, no. 1 (1977), 69–89.

RULE NUMBER NINE

Russell D. Archibald, *Managing High Technology Programs and Projects* (New York: Wiley, 1976).

Michael K. Badawy, *Developing Managerial Skills in Engineers and Scientists* (New York: Van Nostrand Reinhold, 1982).

James M. Kouzes and Barry Z. Posner, *The Leadership Challenge: How to Get Extraordinary Things Done in Organizations* (San Francisco: Jossey-Bass, 1987).

W. Alan Randolph, *Understanding and Managing Organizational Behavior: A Developmental Perspective* (Homewood, Ill.: Richard D. Irwin, 1985.)

Gary A. Yukl, *Leadership in Organizations* (Englewood Cliffs, N.J.: Prentice-Hall, 1981).

RULE NUMBER TEN

James Adams, *Conceptual Blockbusting* (Stanford, Calif.: Stanford Alumni Association, 1974).

H. Joseph Reitz, *Behavior in Organizations* (Homewood, Ill.: Richard D. Irwin, 1977).

Albert Shapero, *Managing Professional People: Understanding Creative Performance* (New York: Free Press, 1985).

ACKNOWLEDGMENTS

ACKNOWLEDGMENTS

It is with pleasure that we acknowledge the insights, information, and encouragement afforded us by others. First, to the thousands of people who have attended our Project Planning and Management seminars; as we wrote this book, we had you in mind.

A special thanks to the following colleagues who reviewed the entire manuscript and provided additional examples, informative suggestions, and good cheer:

Cheryl Breetwor
President
ShareData, Inc.
Sunnyvale, California

Kim Detiveaux
Management Development
Representative
Pacific Gas & Electric
Company
San Francisco, California

Stephen Carter
President
Carter, Goble Associates,
Inc.
Columbia, South Carolina

John Harrison
Manager, Banking and
Financial Planning
Sunkist Growers, Inc.
Van Nuys, California

Randy Lamkin
  Management Development
    Director
  Richland Memorial Hospital
  Columbia, South Carolina

Ronald Luman
  Missile Analysis Supervisor
  Applied Physics Laboratory
  Johns Hopkins University
  Laurel, Maryland

Robert Phillips
  President
  Health Business
    Development Associates
    Inc.
  Emeryville, California

Victor Robinson
  Engineering Manager
  Mid-West Conveyor
    Company
  Kansas City, Kansas

Jeff Samet
  Director, Downtown Office
    Marketing
  City of Baltimore
  Baltimore, Maryland

George W. Summerson, Jr.
  Division Manager
  Hoechst-Roussel
    Pharmaceutical, Inc.
  Columbia, South Carolina

Mark Tager
  President
  Great Performance, Inc.
  Chicago, Illinois

Charles White
  Executive Director
  Sigma Phi Epsilon Fraternity
  Richmond, Virginia

Steve Willard
  President
  Steve Willard and Associates
  Portland, Oregon

Linda Wilshusen
  Executive Director
  Transportation Commission
  Santa Cruz County
  Santa Cruz, California

We also want to thank Ken Blanchard, Pat Zigarmi, and Drea Zigarmi (all of Blanchard Training and Development), Gary Powell (University of Connecticut), Jim Kouzes (Santa Clara University), and Brian Robinson (Santa Clara University). We have learned a great deal from them in joint research efforts and management development seminars. They are sure to recognize their handiwork in this material. Of course, all responsibility for any shortcomings remain ours.

A very special and grateful note of appreciation to Jackie Schmidt-Posner, Ruth Anne Randolph, and Elizabeth Caravelli. Jackie and Ruth Anne read the entire manuscript and offered both substantive and editorial suggestions. Liz typed and retyped the manuscript with remarkable efficiency and care. Thank you.

Finally, this project was tough, challenging, and fun. We both spent considerable effort to define and clarify our goals and objectives, to keep on schedule, to recognize each other's strengths and tensions, to find common ground, to be honest with each other, and to provide support, encouragement, and critical reflections. We determined the order of authors by a flip of the coin. We think we got the job done!

ABOUT THE AUTHORS

ABOUT THE AUTHORS

W. ALAN RANDOLPH

W. Alan Randolph is on the management faculty in the College of Business Administration at the University of South Carolina in Columbia, South Carolina. He is a member of the Core Faculty for the M.B.A. program and also teaches in the Master of International Business Program. Alan is an active trainer in the school's Management Development Center. He has designed and delivered programs on such topics as leadership, project management, group skills and assertive-communications.

Alan is also a Senior Associate with Blanchard Training and Development (home of *The One Minute Manager*) located in San Diego. He designs and conducts seminars on Situational Leadership, One Minute Management, and Productivity Improvement projects. He has managed ongoing management and productivity improvement projects with a number of organizations—most recently the City of Indianapolis Department of Public Works, Pacific Gas & Electric Company, and Pittsburg and Midway Coal Mining Company. He is often called upon as a consultant and trainer in effective project planning and management. Recently, he has consulted with Siemens Medical Systems, Allied Chemical Corporation, E. I. DuPont Company, Digital Equipment Corporation, Gen Rad Corporation, and the Veterans Administration. He has trained literally thousands of managers in the skills of getting the job done through effective project planning and management.

Alan has authored two books—*The Organization Game* (Scott-

Foresman, 1985) and *Understanding and Managing Organizational Behavior* (Irwin, 1985). He has also published over 60 monographs and articles in such scholarly and practitioner-oriented journals as *California Management Review, Human Resources Management, Personnel Psychology, Journal of Applied Psychology, Academy of Management Journal, Human Relations,* and *Group and Organization Studies.*

Alan received the Bachelor of Industrial Engineering degree from Georgia Institute of Technology, and a Master's degree in Personnel and a Ph.D. in Business Administration from the University of Massachusetts. He is incoming President of the Southern Management Association. He is also a member of the Academy of Management, the Organizational Behavior Teaching Society, and Tau Beta Pi, and was selected to Who's Who in American Colleges and Universities, and the Outstanding Young Men of America.

BARRY Z. POSNER

Barry Z. Posner is the Director of Graduate Business Programs and associate professor of management at the Leavey School of Business and Administration at Santa Clara University, Santa Clara, California. He has been described as an ''outstanding teacher and educator'' and has received the President's Distinguished Faculty Award and the Outstanding Young Men in America award. He is also academic director for the university's Executive Development Center.

Barry is an internationally recognized management educator. He has planned and participated in management development programs for IBM, Lockheed, ITT, FMC, the American Management Association, the U.S. Chamber of Commerce, the American Electronics Association, Measurex, Shaklee Corporation, the Internal Revenue Service, St. John's Hospital and Medical Center, the Instituto de Administration Cientifica de las Empresas in Mexico City, and the Australian Institute of Management. In addition to project management, his training programs include leadership, conflict management, and team building.

Barry is an active organizational researcher who has published over 50 articles in a variety of professional journals. For the American Management Association he wrote two monographs, *Managerial Values and Expectations* and *Managerial Values in Perspective.* His latest book, about how to get extraordinary things done in organizations, is titled *The Leadership Challenge* (San Francisco: Jossey-Bass, 1987). Barry also serves on the board of directors of several private and nonprofit organizations. He is the president of the Western Academy of Management.

Barry received a bachelor's degree from the University of California at Santa Barbara, a master's degree from Ohio State University, and a Ph.D. in business administration from the University of Massachusetts. He is a member of the Academy of Management, the American Psychological Association, the Engineering Management Society, the Organization Behavior Teaching Society, and Beta Gamma Sigma.

INDEX

INDEX